GW00585190

From Contempt To Curiosity

Creating the Conditions
for Groups to Collaborate

USING CLEAN LANGUAGE
& SYSTEMIC MODELLING™

CAITLIN WALKER

CLEAN PUBLISHING

From Contempt to Curiosity
Creating Conditions for Groups to Collaborate
Using Clean Language and Systemic Modelling™

by Caitlin Walker

Published by Clean Publishing
14 Anson Grove,
Portchester, Fareham,
Hampshire, England, PO16 8JG

Printed in Great Britain by Cedar Group
Cover Design by Marian Way
Illustrations by Steve Whitla

The author asserts the moral right to be identified as the author of this work.

ISBN: 978-0-9574866-1-4

Systemic Modelling™ is a trademark of Training Attention Ltd.

www.trainingattention.co.uk

Contents

Acknowledgements

I'd like to begin by acknowledging the writing of Kurt Vonnegut Junior. Reading his books in my teenage years inspired me to take my childish concerns about the world and want to do something about them. Similarly, the lyrics, music and concerts of Billy Bragg demonstrated to me the possibility of changing narratives, in the moment, through stories, songs and action.

The teachings of David Grove, and his processes of Clean Language, Clean Space and Emergent Knowledge are the foundation that the work in this book is built on. I miss him still and hope he would be proud that I finally put pen to paper.

I'll be eternally grateful to Penny Tompkins and James Lawley for introducing me to David, for their dedication to modelling his work and making it available to so many and for their skill as teachers. They took me under their wing and patiently guided me along my path; I'd like to thank them for their vision and compassion.

I'd like to acknowledge my fellow learners, clients, colleagues and playmates, those whose names appear in these stories as well as those I've yet to write about.

For the mammoth task of getting the stories out of my head and onto paper, I'd like to acknowledge: Rachel Dunscombe for putting together TEDx Merseyside and helping me to see how useful these stories were for other people; Richard Stacey, Lesley Symons, Tamsin Hartley, Emily Walker, Sue Sharp and Sarah Smith for listening to the stories, asking 'beginner's mind' questions and helping me to transcribe and collate them; and Marian Way for inspiring me to feel capable of overcoming my dyslexic fears and helping me turn those precious stories into a written and readable book. I'd like also like to thank Steve Whitla for producing the illustrations that help to bring the words to life.

Finally, I'd like to thank my family for their support, good humour and love which sustain everything.

Foreword

All too often a breakthrough concept is presented as a miraculous apparition without history or complications, the story of its development shrouded in myth. The resulting sanitised version often feels too good to be true.

Systemic Modelling™ is such a breakthrough concept in human interaction. Fortunately, in this case, Caitlin Walker takes us through the evolution of her work from its source in the Clean Language of David Grove to the formalisation of Systemic Modelling™ and her work in business and educational settings. We are given a real insight into the experiences that have informed her ideas, models and principles, along with a good grounding in what has and hasn't worked.

I know from my own experience that this work is important and enduring; Caitlin's early work in business, which she explores in Chapter 3, also marks the beginning of my own journey with Clean Language. I was working for that Knowledge Management focussed Software Company as they made use of Clean Language in meetings and to develop metaphors for internal and external communication. The 'flatty-sidey' metaphor she helped me to develop, around one of our products, underpinned the later founding of my company.

Clean questions are now a crucial part of our sales approach, and the healthy collaborative environment, which results from using Clean Language, metaphor and Systemic Modelling™ internally, has allowed us to thrive even as our industry has been changing significantly.

Clean Language ensures respectful, meaningful communication using only a handful of well-specified questions. Anyone can do it, regardless of aptitude and background, and this creates an attitude of genuine and respectful curiosity that delivers results across a wide array of business situations. We use it to help us work at our best as individuals, as well as to ensure strong, focused teamwork. When working with customers it helps us quickly understand situations and deploy our products and expertise in a respectful but powerful way.

Software companies frequently fracture into different camps, often driven by very different personalities: people who like programming all day versus sales people who enjoy talking to people all day. Systemic Modelling™ levels the playing field, by giving everyone a strong and confident voice, regardless of the topic, as well as helping those voices to be expressed in a way that's collaborative rather than confrontational. The resulting cross-departmental collaboration delivers measurable business impact on a regular basis on everything from sales situations, to customer support, to internal processes. It really is hard to over-emphasise the benefits of such a simple tool in empowering everyone to contribute, confidently putting their views forward.

Over the years I've come to realise that this is all part of a much wider, and much-needed trend towards a more human, respectful work environment. Teams are composed of people, and the relationships between people are a key aspect of both organisational effectiveness and individual wellbeing.

An unexpected benefit from this journey has been that the tools are just as effective in our personal lives. It really has helped us be better as parents and partners.

Systemic Modelling™ has the ability to gently, albeit firmly, transform the health of any organisation and this book is an invaluable tool for business leaders, educators and for parents who want to make the most of the people they work, learn and live with.

Simon Coles
CEO and Co-Founder, Amphora Research Systems Ltd.
13th February 2014

Prologue

This book is all about attention. It explores how the quality of the attention we pay to ourselves, to the stories we hear, to the people we meet and to the world at large, profoundly affects the things we are able to think and therefore the things we are able to do.

This is my story about developing Systemic Modelling™, a process for improving the quality of attention we give to the relationships we make and the communities we build together.

It centres around a questioning technique called Clean Language, developed by psychotherapist David Grove and shows, through a series of stories, how this simple, powerful approach can enhance business processes, team work, classrooms, partnerships and communication.

Using Systemic Modelling™ with individuals in groups enables them to:

- Understand better where each of them is coming from.
- Spend less time making assumptions and being in conflict.
- Spend more time in appreciation and wondering what they'd each like to have happen.
- Be interested in untapped resources.
- Make better use of the intelligence and experience of each person in the group.
- Form a network of attention that has group level intelligence.
- Make the changes they need to make, now, in this moment.
- Be more inspired and capable.

A core value of this approach is that whatever you're doing with your clients, you're training them to do for themselves. It requires you to engage in ego-less leadership, holding your clients to their own outcomes rather than to yours;

trusting the wisdom in their system over your desire for them to change in specific ways.

It's not a great process for imposing ideas or bringing people into line. It doesn't help to silence dissent or cover up mistakes. It's more likely to call forth challenge and create space for new information. It can feel scary and out of control.

But, as the facilitator pays exquisite attention to the individuals in the room and supports those individuals to pay exquisite attention to one another, a gentle intelligent network emerges that contains and transcends the group.

Within this network people accept themselves as they are and are open to the possibility that they could change. They create the space for acknowledging what has happened and for wondering what they'd like to have happen. They develop the confidence for navigating right into the heart of their conflict and uncovering the fiercely held values that can be found there. They make assumptions, suffer from premature evaluation, make mistakes and then encourage each other in playful humour and forgiveness. They acknowledge their metaphors and stories, their social norms and family narratives and understand how these have served to help them make sense of their complex world. And at the same time they come to realise that none of these stories are really true.

This is a compassionate process for helping a group to become its own appreciative audience. It's a rigorous process for holding a group to its highest values. And it's fun and infectious and easy to adopt, if that's something that you'd like to have happen.

Introduction

Growing up in different continents and reflecting on how social rules, narratives and norms are formed and reformed.

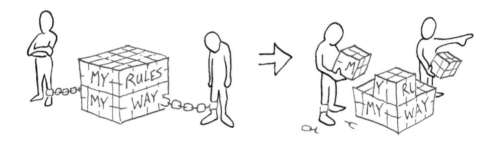

My story really began when I arrived at a new school, in a new country on a new continent and started trying to fit in all over again. I was born in Nigeria and schooled in the United Kingdom so this school in Sacramento, California was on my third continent in nine years. I made my first friend, Twoey, who showed me around, helped me work out how the school day was organised and hung out with me at playtime. Children stared at us and whispered and I assumed it was because I was new and British. But I soon realised it was because I was breaking an unwritten rule.

> *You shouldn't play with Twoey.*
> *Why not?*
> *He's a nigger.*
> *What's that?*
> *He's black.*
> *So what?*
> *Well you just can't play with him that's all.*
> *But that's stupid.*

Once it was brought to my attention, I started to see the segregation in the classes and the playground and on the bus. It made me feel awkward and confused. I didn't know how to play this game and the other kids couldn't see that the rules they were playing by weren't true – they were just made up. Of course, I didn't know what to do with these thoughts just then – but they kept my attention.

As a young adult, I was fascinated by the idea of different cultures having different ways of experiencing the world. I wondered how time could be a conveyor belt for some people, with each day needing to be filled up or it would pass by, while for others a day could be like a pulse or a cycle with choices only existing in the here and now. I wondered how we could ever truly understand each other. I went on to study anthropology and linguistics at the School of Oriental and African Studies and I discovered how difficult it is to truly understand another culture without first understanding your own unconscious rules. And it's difficult to uncover your own unconscious unspoken rules when you're using them to do the uncovering.

It's difficult to uncover your own unconscious unspoken rules when you're using them to do the uncovering.

I wanted to find a process for inquiring into one another's experience and getting fresh information without projecting our own internal worlds onto one another. I hoped that if I could find such a process then I could uncover my own rules and be freer of them. I hoped that I could connect with other people in a more human way. I hoped that if groups of people could stop telling the same tales over and over again and consider what other stories were possible then we could make up new ways of being together.

Patterns, Behaviours and Attention

One of the jobs that paid my way through university was as a weekend youth worker in an inner city community garden. This was a space where diverse groups of young people were trying to share one territory and a diverse group of youth workers were trying to facilitate the process. A great starting place to see unconscious and conscious social rules in action. I began by observing people's behaviours, kids and youth workers, tracking patterns that could give me a clue to rules I could explore.

Something that caught my attention early on was that when we had to call the police to an incident, it was nearly always on the Sunday, while Saturdays went off without many incidents. People remarked on it but no-one knew why. I wondered if I could find out what was making the difference and I quietly observed the park when it ran smoothly, observed trouble as it kicked off and looked for differences in people's behaviour. The pattern was that it depended on who was in charge of the park.

Our Saturday and Sunday lead youth workers had very different behaviours when they were running the garden. The Sunday worker was often trying to get the kids to join in an idea she had or to stop what they were doing. She was either right in there with them or out of sight completely. The Saturday worker was more detached with the kids, observing and supporting them rather than joining in. She was almost always in sight but when I tried to interview her, she would often disappear off for a few minutes before coming back again.

I interviewed them to find out where their attention was when they were at work and how they thought about their roles. The Saturday worker described herself as keeping harmony in the park. She noted a range of sounds that indicated happy play and a safe park. A different range of sounds: a shift in tone; a sudden silence; the arrival of new voices, meant she needed to investigate.

The moment she heard these changes in sound, she would move quickly and gently to observe, intervene and get everyone back on track. This strategy worked well no matter where she was on site and was easily learnable.

The Sunday worker described her role as like that of a security guard. She had a visual map of the garden and said she knew who to look out for as potential trouble and where things were likely to kick off. The terrain in the park was hilly and the kids often hung out in nooks and crannies, which meant she couldn't see trouble until it was in full swing, erupting from the hidden areas, and so was often too late to stop it. This worker also smoked and was regularly off-site for brief periods, which lessened her ability to keep an eye on the changing moods in the garden. Although her strategy would be great in a different context it wasn't as useful as that of her colleague for keeping the park safe and under control.

Once I had access to their thoughts and behaviours, it was time to change my own – to copy the Saturday 'model' and adopt it myself. Then, when I was at work on a Sunday, I could help keep trouble to a minimum too.

I started observing all sorts of models, how different taxi drivers chose their routes, how lecturers listened to and answered student questions, how the kids got groups of friends to follow their games rather than someone else's. I would practise modelling whenever an opportunity presented itself.

I stayed in the field of cognitive linguistics, researching how people make meaning out of the spoken word. Then, about three years into my postgraduate research I was invited by two mentors of mine, Penny Tompkins and James Lawley, to observe the Maori psychotherapist, David Grove, at work. They said he was able to do amazing things with a technique he called Clean Language. They were studying him to build up their model of what he was doing and to find out whether his approach could be replicated and taught to others working in this field. They said he used 'clean' questions to help clients develop metaphors for their psychological symptoms and to give them greater access to information that was previously unconscious. This sounded right up my street.

David Grove, Clean Questions and Metaphors

I turned up at a hotel in London where David was working with a client at the front of the room. The client said she had an issue with speaking in public – that she panicked and couldn't breathe and that this was affecting her ability to progress at work.

David: **What would you like to have happen?**
Client: To be able to do public speaking without panicking.
David: **And is there anything else about** public speaking without panicking?
Client: It's like I can't *(touching her chest)* … I can't breathe.
David: **And when** you can't breathe, **what kind of** can't breathe?
Client: It's like my breath keeps getting lost.
David: **And when** your breath keeps getting lost, **whereabouts is** getting lost?
Client: It's like there's a hole in my chest.
David: **Anything else about that** hole?
Client: It's a real hole and I'm frozen.
David: **What kind of** frozen?
Client: I can't breathe; I'm by the door.
David: **And** by the door, can't breathe, frozen … **and is there anything else?**
Client: The hole is in dad's head. I want to shout but I'm frozen.

As I watched and listened, David gently helped this woman to pay attention to her symptom until she made links between not being able to breathe when she had something important to say in public and an early childhood trauma in which she'd seen her father shoot himself and had been unable to use her voice to call for help or to stop him.

David's approach allowed her to develop metaphors for aspects of her experience and build up a whole landscape in which she could make better sense of her unconscious thoughts, feelings and physiological responses. Within this landscape she found resources and strengths and was able to unfreeze her frozen inner child and to reintegrate her lost voice. By the end of the session, she was commenting on her experience rather than being locked in the trauma.

She was still the same woman but she held herself differently, breathed differently, had more access to her whole body; she had transformed in front of our eyes. Most impressively, David had run the whole session using only her words and her gestures and a tiny handful of these clean questions. I was amazed. It seemed like magic.

The big difference between what he was doing with his client and what I

"In asking a [clean] question we do not impose upon the client any value, construct or presupposition about what he should answer."
— *David Grove and Basil Panzer*

had been trying to do in the community garden, was that he was helping her to uncover her own model rather than trying to create the model for her. The clean questions helped her to explore her experience, the unconscious links between her past and her present, with no interpretation coming from him.

This was already resonating with my inner nine-year-old and I could feel the potential for this work.

David invited the audience to get into pairs, to ask each other:

What would you like to have happen?

… and then to expand our partners' answers using their exact words and just these three clean questions:

What kind of … ?
Where is that … ?
Is there anything else about … ?

The guy next to me said, "Can I work with you?" And I thought, "Oh no, what a boring looking man." He was all grey in demeanour. But I agreed and I ran the process with him and then he asked me:

Partner: **What would you like to have happen?**
Me: *(Using my hand...)* I need to find my path.
Partner: **What kind of** path **is that?**
Me: It's compelling *(pointing off to the side)*.
Partner: **Where is that** path?

As I started to indicate my path again, I realised that there were two paths: one in front of me which was the way I had been going and one off to the side called my compelling path.

Me: Over here.
Partner: **Is there anything else about that** path?
Me: It's not the direction I've been going in.

I stood there looking at my two hands and all sorts of things started to fall into place. I could now understand why I was so miserable at university and in my personal life. Neither of these areas of my life were compelling, just things I'd agreed to do and felt duty bound to persist with. I would never be happy if I continued on this path and having this revealed so clearly changed everything.

In three questions, a stranger I hadn't even wanted to work with had helped me to uncover an unconscious model for what I really wanted next in my life. If a beginner could help me to get to that deep insight with only three clean questions, this process must be easy to learn and easy to put into practice. Could this be the process I was looking for?

The event ended, I went upstairs to the hotel lobby and sat at the bar in a daze for a while, my gin and tonic remaining untouched. I had the clearest vision. I could see this Clean Language stuff spreading out through community gardens, schools, workplaces, countries ... casting a different quality of light on our communication and on our communities. This was my compelling path: to help take this stuff to places where it needed to be taken; to re-examine our rules for living and learning together; to listen to the stories we tell ourselves and make sure they are fit for purpose. I sat there until the bar closed, then I went home and the next morning I got up, ended my on-off relationship of 12 years, left my linguistic research and walked away from everything that wasn't compelling.

CHAPTER 1

Training Attention

*Using clean questions to create models
of subjective experience*

I decided that I'd do whatever it took to find out more about Clean Language, David Grove and how I could use this approach in my own work. So I turned up at Penny and James's door and, after a couple of questions to check I was serious, they agreed to have me along on their journey of finding out what David was doing and how we could teach it to others.

I began inviting friends and colleagues around to my house and offering to help them explore their skills, experiences and feeling. These would need to be positive things that they were good at, or felt good about, since we were all beginners and needed to be able to make mistakes.

The Clean Practice Group

I wrote David's clean questions out, one per card, we sat in a circle, and asked the focus of attention, "What would you like to have happen?" and then each of us in turn would take what the focus said, ask the clean question on our card and see what happened. We started with Guy as the focus.

A: **What would you like to have happen?**
Guy: I'd like to get more in touch with my feelings so that I can write better
          songs about them.
B: **What kind of** feelings?
Guy: Deep ones.
C: **And is there anything else about those** deep feelings?
Guy: They're inside me.
D: **And where** inside me?
Guy: Deep in my heart.
E: **And do those feelings have a size or a shape?**
Guy: Yes it's like this *(cups his hands together)*.
F: **And when it's** like this, **that's like what?**
Guy: It's an onion, a rich red onion.

And we were off... We all learned to ask the questions and to gently and slowly help one another to explore our models for things we were good at or aspects of ourselves that we wanted to find out more about. When asked clean questions, people often came up with spontaneous, self-generated metaphors that encapsulated their experience. David Grove says that these metaphors mediate between the conscious and unconscious and, just like my *compelling path*, they can be hugely meaningful. Guy says he still uses the onion metaphor to this day, that it's more relevant to his song writing now than ever.

> Metaphors mediate between the conscious and unconscious.
> — *David Grove*

An important member of these front room practice sessions was a participant from one of Penny and James's early Clean Language and Metaphor Therapy trainings, Dee Berridge. She and I were so keen to become skilled at clean questions that we dedicated every single Wednesday, for three years, to practising our clean modelling skills.

We assisted on Penny and James's 'Grovian Metaphor Therapy' trainings. We arranged modelling retreats with David to experience his work first-hand and to unpack more of his magic. We ate, slept and breathed clean questions, metaphors and modelling.

We decided to set up a Clean Practice Group. We didn't want this to be a place where people presented ideas while others listened; we wanted it to be a training ground with everyone engaged in active practice, feedback, learning and improvement. There was a process to the way we ran the group. We would take something we'd learned from David, or an idea we'd had, and then we'd explore and practise it with one another and feed back on our own experience. Next we'd try the same things out with friends or colleagues and get their feedback. Finally, we'd take whatever we had learned and turn it into a more polished training exercise for our newly formed Clean Practice Group and find out how it worked with a group of people.

Working With Individuals

Although we were nowhere near as skilled as David, we began taking on our own clients and were soon helping individuals and groups uncover metaphors for their symptoms. As their metaphors expanded, updated and transformed, so did their corresponding experience in the world.

One of the most inspiring things about collaborating with Dee was that neither of us limited the potential scope for these ideas. Whatever occurred to us, we'd take to the other and start modelling it. One day she asked whether we could use clean questions to model pain as a friend of hers was suffering. We didn't know if it would be effective but we had a go. I'd had a pain in my wrist since I was 17 so we started modelling that. I said it felt like a dark crack in a rock face so Dee asked me some clean questions about the 'crack' and the 'dark' and developed the metaphor. I realised that the crack changed shape and was sometimes deep and sometimes shallow. The deeper it was the more my wrist hurt. Afterwards, I began to notice when the crack felt worse and what eased it. With the metaphor in mind I quickly realised that tomatoes and orange juice made it worse and worked out that I needed to eat a more alkaline diet. My metaphor was giving me more access to knowledge that was contained in my body.

Having had a go ourselves, we invited Dee's friend round and asked her some clean questions to help build up a model of her pain.

Dee: **Your pain is like what?**
Friend: A gripping.
Dee: **Where is that** gripping?
Friend: In the small of my back.
Dee: **Is there anything else about** gripping?
Friend: It's hard.
Dee: Hard **like what?**
Friend: Like a fist.
Caitlin: **And** gripping, in the small of your back, like a fist, **and is there anything else about that** fist?
Friend: It was a hand.
Caitlin: **What kind of** hand?
Friend: A supportive hand, but then it got too tight.
Caitlin: **And** a supportive hand **and** got too tight. **And when** supportive, **is there anything else about** supportive?
Friend: It's my Mum's hand.

… and then she was talking about how ill she was as a child … how her mum would keep her on the sofa and stroke her hair and make a fuss of her … and how that had turned from something supportive to a role she had started to play out in her family. Her back pain was now so bad that she spent a lot of the day on the sofa, unable to look after her own child.

Dee and I spent a few sessions helping this friend to expand her model of the fist, her back and the support she'd had from her mother. The fist loosened its grip and she had more access to movement. Instead of the metaphor running her, she was able to see it within it's own context and make sense of the pattern that she was replaying.

From here we created a process for working with physical well-being and took it to the practice group to test its impact.

Idea-Self-Other-Group

This pattern of having an idea, applying it to ourselves, testing it on others and then developing a group learning process defined the next three years and was just the sort of thing I'd hoped for when I first saw David working. We were helping people to have access to their unconscious rules without projecting our own experience on one another. Once people had access to those rules, the rules themselves seemed more open to transformation and updating. When we ran this process at a group level it started to become the culture of that group to explore and update rules.

> We were helping people to have access to their unconscious rules without projecting our own experience on one another.

As well as making models of people's experience, Dee and I became interested in the patterns we had for actually doing the modelling. We wanted to do some meta-modelling – to explore the very way that we were modelling other people. The questions themselves might be clean but which questions we asked and which bit of a client's experience we focussed on was still very much based on the modeller. We turned our attention to what was going on for the person doing the modelling.

- Where was our attention when we were working?
- How did we remember what someone had or hadn't said?
- How did the way we were remembering information impact on what questions we asked next?

For example, I'm able to remember, word for word, a lot of what someone might say and then to repeat it back verbatim. Dee had to practise a lot in order to be able to track back through all the spoken words but was more able to pick up on the energy of a session and know where would be a good place to put someone's attention. We asked one another a few clean questions to try to work out the differences between us but realised we needed to be doing it live.

Since Dee and I worked together with our clients on a two-to-one basis, we would be running these different strategies during the same session. We asked one client if it would be OK for Dee and I to model one another in-the-moment to find out how each of us was tracking their information.

I would ask the client a few clean questions to develop their metaphor and then I'd stop and Dee would ask me a few clean questions to find out how I was remembering what the client had said. Then I would ask the client more questions, stop, Dee would model me, and so on.

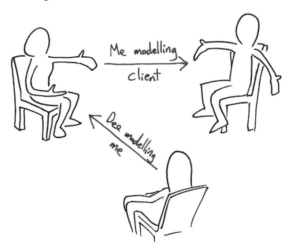

She helped me to realise that I didn't so much hear what the client said, I pictured it in the air around them. The words hung in the air. When the client said something more than once then it became emboldened around them. Once Dee could see how my model worked she was able to have a go at it and see if she could begin remembering like I did. Then we'd swap round and she'd ask the client some questions and I'd find out how she knew which question to ask next. She was almost putting herself in the other person's body and feeling their feelings. She could be inside the metaphor; this was how she detected the richest areas of someone's metaphors.

We took these insights to our practice group and got them to model one another's modelling strategies. Once they each had a model of how they were actually paying attention to their clients they could understand why they were learning some parts of David's work faster than others. The way they paid attention to their clients affected the kind of attention those clients could pay to themselves.

This was an important finding and for almost a year, Dee and I turned our attention to all the different things that can affect how we pay attention to others.

We started with memory strategies and created exercises for mo. longer term memory. We would take lists of words, read them out how they were trying to remember them. Some would repeat the wc over in their own voice, others would make pictures of them and some link them in a story. We noticed that some people's memory strategies m. .c it easier for them to be cleaner than those of others. For example, if someone remembered the list of words by making pictures of them and putting them into a context, we often found that, as they listened to clients' words and metaphors, they made their own pictures and created a context around what the client was saying too. With this strategy it would be easy to think the picture content came from the client and unwittingly ask 'unclean' questions based on that. So they had to learn to distinguish between what they'd actually heard and what they'd added in to make it memorable.

The fact that I remembered what was said simply as written words in space meant I was unlikely to put in 'unclean' details or add in my own words. However, I was also busy keeping all of that information in my memory and so paying a lot less attention to voice tone and feelings etc.

A really exciting discovery was that people who remembered words in our memory games by repeating them often felt overloaded by clients who gave long answers because it was hard to hold large tracts of information in mind with this strategy. We could then use all of this learning to help one another build really effective strategies for listening to others and remembering what had actually been said and becoming better clean modellers.

Dee and I were using a handful, though not all, of the clean questions that were used by David Grove. We used a model, devised by Penny and James, to show where we were training our attention.

Training attention on...

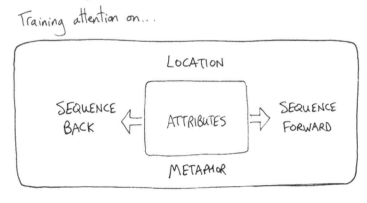

And these were the main questions we were asking...

The big area we were working on was the attention and state and skills required to do this clean modelling. The crux of what we were doing was encapsulated in a model I developed while training clean modelling in the north-west of England with Chris Grimsley. Chris is an excellent trainer with a knack of taking complex processes and making them easily accessible to groups of 'ordinary folk'. He wanted me to find a simple way of describing the very essence of being a clean modeller. In response I said that it was essentially doing opposing things at the same time:

"While you're listening to the person you are modelling, you need to separate out *what you're actually seeing and hearing* from the *sense you're making of it*. You're distinguishing what is being presented from what is being inferred.

To detect patterns, you have to know some of your own patterns.

"At the same time, you are *detecting patterns in that person* and, in order to do this, you have to *know some of your own patterns*. If you don't know your own patterns you won't be able to tell what is you and what is someone else. For example, I know I talk very quickly and that I like other people to do the same. So if I'm modelling someone who talks slowly I need to remember that it is my pattern that is making me think that they're talking slowly, rather than a pattern that is necessarily significant for them.

"While you're modelling you need to be able to *open your senses* up to the person you're modelling. You need to train your sensory acuity so that you can listen to words *and* spot gestures *and* be in touch with sensations and emotions. While you're opening up your senses you also need to know what the session is for. You need to be *helping that person build useful models* and to keep tying in the information you're picking up and feeding it back to them."

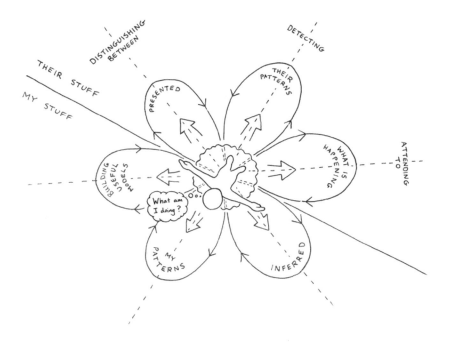

The diagram I drew as I spoke looked like a flower with petals to represent the different facets, so we called it the Flower Model. The idea is that you're always moving between the different petals and that clean questions, curiosity and respect help you to keep in a modelling frame of mind.

In this spirit of experimentation, exploration, trying out new ideas and sharing our experience, Dee and I developed all kinds of new applications for clean questions and metaphors outside of psychotherapy and one-to-one work. We modelled not only memory but also working at our best, learning at our best, time, organisation, confidence, lying... you name it, we modelled it. We were mainly having a really good time but looking back this was just as rigorous as much of my postgraduate research and very engaging.

There were also some highly practical outputs and tools. For example, as Dee and I came to understand how different our internal worlds were, we also understood why we frequently had different expectations and experiences of the same event and how come we often misunderstood what the other person meant. We wanted to work with our differences and, almost by accident, we developed the three key tools that have come to underpin this whole approach.

Before we started an event, whether it was a client session or a piece of training, we would ask each other how we wanted the event to go and what we expected from one another. We'd write up our outcomes on a flip chart and use them to remind us to keep the other person's outcomes in mind as well as our own.

We asked it both ways round and then worked out what we needed to do to support one other to do the best job we could. I later came to call this approach a Clean Set Up.

Clean Set Up:
Using Clean Questions to Create Shared Outcomes

Here's an example of a Clean Set Up which Dee and I did to prepare for a training we were running together:

Dee

Caitlin: **For this training to go just the way you'd like, it will be like what?**

Dee: The training will be like a brilliant firework display with the crowd mesmerised by their own internal worlds as well as the processes we are teaching.

Caitlin: **And when it's** like a brilliant firework display **and** the crowd is mesmerised, **what will you see or hear?**

Dee: I'll hear lots of Ooohs and Aahs and see people in trance.

Caitlin: **For this training to go like that, you'll be like what?**

Dee: I'm the orchestrator of the fireworks.

Caitlin: **And when** you're the orchestrator of the fireworks, **what will *I* see or hear?**

Dee: I'll be keeping us to time and reminding the group when to move on.

Caitlin: **What support or resources will you need?**

Dee: I need space to build anticipation and make sure the rockets look great against a dark sky.

Caitlin: **What will you see or hear?**

Dee: I need times when you'll sit quietly and let the sky clear. I'll stand up in front of the flip chart a few moments before I speak.

Caitlin

Dee: **For this training to go just the way you'd like, it will be like what?**

Caitlin: I'd like the training to be like starting off gently passing a ball back and forth around the circle getting a feel for people's strengths. Then increasing the pace so that people will start passing the ball between themselves.

Dee: **And when it's like that, what will you see or hear?**

Caitlin: I'll know it's working when they're the ones who start asking clean questions.

Dee: **For the training to go like that, you'll be like what?**

Caitlin: I'd like to be a hands-off coach. Very observant and ensuring that everyone is getting a chance to get their hands on the ball.

Dee: **And when you're** a hands-off coach **and** ensuring everyone is getting a chance to get their hands on the ball, **what will I see or hear?**

Caitlin: You'll see me mainly asking questions and holding back from giving explanations.

Dee: **What support or resources will you need?**

Caitlin: For this to happen I need you to take over at times so that I can watch
          without taking part and work out who needs attention.

Dee: **What will I see or hear when you need me to take over?**

Caitlin: Can I give you a nod when I need you?

Once we'd done our Clean Set Up, we would talk practically about how we'd
pull the two outcome metaphors together and decide who was going to do what
when. Our expectations were aligned and our heads were in the right space to
start. We would either use this process as a two-minute 'state setter' or we could
take a new project and use the process for an hour to get really clear about what
each of us wanted to have happen.

   As well as using the Clean Set Up to prepare for an event and to get shared
outcomes, we regularly set ourselves little tasks to develop our skills and
flexibility. We called these our 'Developmental Tasks'.

Developmental Tasks

Having a Developmental Task
meant doing something outside
of our normal patterns – such
as taking on another person's
memory strategy to feel how
it worked. It wasn't just self-
discovery; it was ongoing self
development and developing
flexibility. Sometimes we decided
on our own Developmental Tasks
and at other times we came up
with something for the other to
practise.

   For example, Dee asked me
to practise being more time-
focussed when we were training
and to do things in the order we'd agreed. Every time I succeeded she'd give me a
subtle thumbs-up.

I asked her to deliberately interrupt me and set her rocket off in the middle of me talking. This was challenging for her because it stretched her rule about waiting for someone to finish before speaking. When she did it, I'd sit down and give her the space she needed and she learned to take up more space publicly.

Sometimes we found we'd chosen the wrong task – it didn't help us to develop the flexibility we'd been hoping for. And sometimes we couldn't do the tasks; after all, we were going against patterns of a lifetime – me flitting around all over the place and Dee politely waiting for someone to finish. But by setting these tasks and giving one another feedback afterwards we recognised a higher level of relationship between us and a deep sense of respect. We were being true to ourselves and, at the same time, learning to adjust our behaviour to help the other person be themselves too.

Developmental Tasks should be 'light', short-term and discrete. They should be designed to give you an opportunity to try out something new and learn from it and then create a new outcome based on that learning.

Clean Feedback

Even the way we gave feedback to each other took on a new aspect. We started separating out what we wanted to say to each other into different kinds of information. The first bit of the feedback was simply a description of what had happened without any judgement in it – the evidence. Next we could say what we thought about what had happened or what it meant to us – our inference. Finally we could share the impact this was having on us. Later, this became known as 'Clean Feedback'.

A key piece of the model is that evidence means observable behaviour. A word like 'good' doesn't fit that criteria. So instead of Dee telling me I'd been good at keeping to time and then me having to work out what she meant by 'good', she'd say, "You started three out of five sessions on time and in the right order. I interpreted this as you being supportive and I was much more relaxed during the other two sessions."

Evidence: You started three out of five sessions on time and in the right order.
Inference: You were being supportive.
Impact: I was much more relaxed during the other two sessions.

And instead of saying she'd been more dominant during the training I could say, "When I was talking with one participant for five minutes, you spoke over the top of us and asked who had a different idea to his. I thought you'd realised I'd forgotten about the rest of the group and I felt secure knowing you were keeping an eye on the big picture and keeping the orchestra on track."

Evidence: When I had been talking with one participant for five minutes you spoke over the top of us and asked who had a different idea to his.
Inference: You had realised that I'd forgotten about the rest of the group.
Impact: I felt secure knowing you were keeping an eye on the big picture and keeping the orchestra on track.

We could give feedback to each other about what was working well, what wasn't working so well and what we thought would work better.

The Karma Cycle

These three tools together – Clean Set Up for developing desired outcomes, Developmental Tasks for taking action and Clean Feedback for discovering and reflecting on the impact of our actions – freed us from constantly making assumptions and getting things wrong and instead allowed us to find small compromises that made a huge difference to how well we worked together. Later on we came to call this set of tools the Karma Cycle, from the Sanskrit root kri meaning right action. This cycle can go in different directions so long as each action is observed and reflected upon and the learning is continuous. As we were becoming experts in clean modelling, we were also learning to enter into each new situation in a state of not knowing and curiosity. Over time we called this

process 'becoming a naive expert'. We were learning to balance the patterns that we could detect and the predictions we could make about individuals and groups with the idea that we couldn't ever really know about another person or team or group. What we could do was to ask questions, acknowledge our prejudices and endeavour to become more flexible in our responses to one another.

At this stage of our development I didn't know how important the Karma Cycle was going to become to the development of the larger process of Systemic Modelling™ and in supporting groups to inspire capability in themselves and in one another. This was just Dee and I working out how to apply the processes to ourselves before we used them on other people and loving the insights and learning we were having.

Next Steps Along The Path

We were generally working with well-resourced people who were interested in personal and professional development and we were finding it relatively easy to engage our groups in these processes and to gain a reputation that brought us more clients. I looked around for new groups who might not be quite so open to this kind of self-reflection and change. I wanted to find out whether the processes could be transferred to a wider audience who weren't already sold on the idea.

Penny, James, Dee and I came together to help one another to set our personal goals for Clean Language. I wanted to take David's work out into diverse groups, in all walks of life, teach it to them and see what happened. I felt sure that it would be useful but had absolutely no idea why or what would happen. I decided that I was going to stop reading books and learning new models; instead I was going to concentrate on applying clean modelling and just pay attention to whatever emerged. When I was sure I had something worth sharing, then I'd stop and write a book about it.

Penny and James went on to develop Symbolic Modelling, their brilliant model of David's approach for facilitating self-modelling with individuals. Dee combined her exquisite clean coaching with producing her extraordinary art. And this book is the story of what happened to me along my compelling path, some of the people I met, the metaphors we uncovered, the changes that occurred and some of the possible applications for this amazingly simple process.

CHAPTER 2

Moving from Contempt to Curiosity

Working cleanly with groups of disaffected inner-city teenagers

I started looking around for something that would keep my path compelling and I stumbled across this job with the Home Office:

... working with ten of the most disruptive 11to14-year-olds, 'at risk' of becoming offenders, from 'failing' schools in East London and persuading them to voluntarily attend nine hours of after-school tuition to address their educational and behavioural needs. The longer term aim being that they re-join the mainstream education system and realise their potential.

This got my attention. Would I be able to bring my youth work and my clean modelling skills together and get kids who disrupted every classroom they entered, attended school one day in ten and were known to the police for violent, criminal behaviour, to engage in modelling? What would I need to do so that they would choose for three hours, three times a week after school, to come along to sessions that aimed to improve their behaviour and literacy skills?

Contempt

I applied for the job, got it and during the induction I listened to the leaders of the project and their different ideas about these children and their families. Some felt that the kids were 'bad' and needed 'disciplining'; others felt they were 'helpless' and needed 'rescuing' and would be OK if it wasn't for their upbringing. They talked about giving the kids incentives to come along, almost bribing them into self-development. No one talked about the children as if they were capable or creative or able to think for themselves. It was as though I was being encouraged to hold them in contempt before I had even met them.

I wondered how the school approached these children and during my first visit I found out. I was waiting outside the staffroom when I noticed a woman standing over a child with her face right next to his. He was sobbing and she was hissing in his face, "Just wait till your father gets here. He's going to give you what for. If you think this is bad, wait till he gets you home. He'll sort you out."

I was shocked and frightened. When my contact came out, I said, "I've just witnessed an incident with that woman and that boy." She said, "Oh, with the deputy head?"

This woman wasn't a parent. She was the deputy head. I didn't know what the child had or hadn't done but he clearly wasn't doing anything right then but crying. There was no apparent care or compassion, just vitriol from a head of the school 'family'.

I don't know about you, but if that level of vitriol was being aimed at me, I wouldn't be learning anything. I would either have attacked the deputy head or withdrawn into myself and I was 28 years old and had training. If I couldn't manage the situation, why should that kid be able to?

The next time I visited the school, a thuggish looking youth sitting on a table by the door blocked my way and said gruffly, "Who are you?" I told him my name and which member of staff I was visiting and he unblocked my way with a grunt. I asked, "Who are you?" thinking maybe he was a sixth former. "Security." At first I thought he was kidding but he was actually a paid member of staff.

Again I was struck by how nastiness, aggression and casual abuse seemed legitimate in this school. If the kids were going to fit back into the system, they'd have to conform to these kinds of rules. They'd have to accept this kind of treatment. I started to think, "What if the way that they're responding at school is perfect given the situations they find themselves in? What if it's the only way that they're stopping themselves being in the same state as that child in the corridor? What if they are responding to being held in contempt by the people in charge of them?"

I knew from visiting the children in their homes that there was already plenty of contempt coming from parents, relatives and even from the children themselves:

- We can't do anything with her; she's always been bad.
- I don't know why you're bothering with Jake; he's just lazy.
- It's not Arfin's fault; it's those black boys that get him to do bad things.
- I've got an awful temper, Miss. I'm out of control, aren't I Mum?

Curiosity

I started getting curious about how I could approach this situation differently. When David Grove worked one-to-one with clients, he never held the individuals or their symptoms in contempt. He paid exquisite attention to all aspects of their identity and behaviours, equally, welcoming them all to the table. This non-judgemental acceptance and appreciation meant that fragmented parts of the client's psyche were able to recognise what roles they played and what they were trying to achieve and then reorganise themselves back into the whole person in a less toxic way.

I wanted to find a way to hold the young people in the same space of acceptance, respect and curiosity and to find a way that they could hold themselves and one another in that space too.

> I wanted to find a way to hold the young people in a space of acceptance, respect and curiosity and to find a way that they could hold themselves and one another in that space too.

I'd always meant to use clean questions and modelling in my sessions but now I would make them the central theme. I'd pay the kids exquisite attention, ask them some clean questions and elicit metaphors to find out what was important to them. That was my new plan, although I'd have to do it covertly as none of this was in my job description.

The kids, of course, didn't know what I had promised to do in my job description, so we could just start the way I wanted. In my visits to their homes, I introduced myself and the programme using the metaphor of being a brain coach, able to help them find out how their brains worked and how to use them more effectively. I asked, "If this programme were really useful for you, it would be like what?" and "What would you like to have happen?"

The young people were candid about their issues: they had bad tempers; they stuttered; they were disruptive; they felt lost. And they were clear about their outcomes: they wanted to have more self-control; they wanted to improve their reading and writing; they wanted a future they could look forward to. Before the first session I wrote their individual outcomes on a flip chart, using their exact words, ready to see where they wanted to begin.

Modelling Temper

My first group consisted of ten 12-year-old boys. They all turned up for the first session. I got them to set the room up in a circle, showed them the themes they'd asked for and I asked:

Caitlin: **What would you like to have happen first?**
Moses: I want to stop hitting people; I hate my temper.

Most of the boys nodded so we had our first central theme for some clean modelling.

Caitlin: **OK, before you** hit someone**, how do you know it's going to happen?**

Dan: I just switch miss.
Caitlin: **What kind of** switch?
Dan: Fast *(snaps fingers).*
Caitlin: **So you** just switch *(snaps fingers like Dan)*, fast.

Caitlin: **Who's not like that?**
Moses: I go red *(points to chest).*

Caitlin: **What kind of red?**
Moses: Blood red *(taps chest).*

Caitlin: **Who's different again?**
Kile: I don't go red, everything just goes quiet.

Caitlin: **OK, so you** switch *(snaps fingers like Dan)*, **you** go red *(points to Moses' chest)* **and with you** everything just goes quiet … **What kind of quiet?**
Kile: Quiet like I've got headphones in
Caitlin: **And it's** quiet like you've got headphones on.

Whatever they said, I repeated a few of their words, adding a clean question to help them to build up their model gradually. I tried to match their exact words and also the way they said them, as though I were a tape recorder playing back what they'd said. And if they pointed to their chest, I pointed to their chest too as I asked a question about it.

Caitlin: **And who's different again?**
Ben: Me miss. I don't lose it, I get all … *(feet tap and shake)* … I just get away before I explode.
Caitlin: **You** get all *(points to and looks Ben's feet)* **and** get away before you explode. **And is there anything else about** get away?

Ben: I don't even know that I'm doing it.

Caitlin: **And you** don't even know you're doing it.

Caitlin: **And you** go red *(points to Moses' chest)*, **you** switch
    (snaps fingers like Dan), **and you** go quiet, like you've
    got headphones on. **Anything else about those**
    headphones?

Kile: Like big headphones miss. It all goes quiet *(puts
    hands over ears)* like I can't hear anything in my head
    and I can only see the one in front of me … like
    everything else shuts off and the next thing I know is
    people are shouting, someone's lying on the ground and I'm in trouble.

Caitlin: **And** everything goes quiet, only see the one in front, shuts off, then
    someone's lying on the ground and you're in trouble.

Caitlin: **And you, when you** go blood red, **whereabouts is** blood red?

Moses: Right here, trying to get out *(taps chest again)*.

Caitlin: **And** blood red *(points to Moses' chest)*, **and** everything goes quiet **for
    you,** like headphones, **and you** get all *(points
    to Ben's feet)* **…**

Caitlin: **And you** switch *(snaps fingers like Dan)*. **And
    when** switch *(snaps fingers)* **is there anything
    else about** switch *(snaps fingers)*?

Dan: I'm fine, then someone just looks at me wrong
    and I switch *(snap fingers near his left ear)* and
    I take them out.

Caitlin: You're fine, then someone looks at you wrong and you switch *(snaps
    fingers towards his left ear)* … **And as** they look at you wrong and you
    switch, **what kind of** switch *(snaps fingers towards his left ear)*?

Dan: There's no choice, it just happens.

Caitlin: **And there's** no choice **here,** blood red **here** *(points to Moses' chest)*, **…**
    And you get all *(points to Ben's feet)* **…** and get away before you explode.
    And when you get all *(points to feet)*, **what happens just before you** get
    away?

Ben: I can feel it rising *(feet tap frantically and he gestures to his legs)*.

Kile: I've seen him do that when he's vexed, miss. His knees shake and he just goes. Just walks off.

Ben: Yeah, I always leave before I explode

Kile: True miss. He never gets in trouble for fighting.

Dan: Is that why I get done for fighting miss, cause it happens so fast?

Caitlin: **I don't know. Let's find out.**

And that was how we began: one or two clean questions, summarise that child's model and move on; one or two clean questions, summarise the new model, plus the last model and move on. It was similar to what Dee and I had been doing at our practice group but a little bouncier, quite quick and without the hypnotic quality of most clean modelling sessions. I kept the delivery light and kept moving around the group so as to keep them all involved. This turned out to be a necessary condition for creating the group level attention that is so crucial to Systemic Modelling™ but the behaviours were just a lucky consequence of the group I was working with.

I kept the delivery light and kept moving around the group so as to keep them all involved. This turned out to be a necessary condition for creating the group level attention that is so crucial to Systemic Modelling™.

I kept up the questioning until each boy in the group had a mini model of their temper and knew how it started, what it was like at its worst and how it stopped.

While this process was really effective in keeping the group's attention, it can make quite fragmented reading. I've taken one boy's model out of the dialogue and written it up in sequence below. This excerpt can also give an idea of how you might use this process in a one-to-one session.

Caitlin: **When you** go blood red *(gestures at his chest)*, **whereabouts is** blood red?

Moses: *(Gestures by top of chest with one hand as though something's rising and the hand is holding it down.)* It just gets red and I get angry, like my blood's boiling.

Caitlin: **And like** my blood's boiling, **and** red. **And when** my blood's boiling, **what happens just before** it's boiling?

Moses: It's cooler!

Caitlin: **And when it's** cooler, **what kind of** cooler?

Moses: It's like that *(points to a maroon colour in the room)* and it's here *(points an inch lower on his chest)*.

Caitlin: **And** it's *(points to maroon colour)* **and** it's here *(points to lower on his chest)*. **And when** it's here, **what happens before** it's here.

Moses: It's purple *(points to solar plexus)*.

Caitlin: **And before it's** purple, **it's like what?**

Moses: It's blue, like the sky, like my mum. Then I'm cool. *(His whole physiology shifts, he goes still, looks uncharacteristically calm, tilts his head upwards and smiles a gentle relaxed smile. I notice that no-one mocks him, it's as though they are all entranced.)*

Caitlin: **And** cool blue, like the sky, like your mum, **and then** purple here *(points to solar plexus)* **then** here *(points to chest)* **then** blood red and like your blood's boiling – **and then what happens after** blood's boiling?

Moses: I get raj *(enraged)* and I attack, then it's out of me and I run and run until I calm down.

I invited the boys to storyboard their tempers and draw them out on paper, which we put on the walls.

I suggested that between now and the next session, they keep attention on their tempers to find out if these story boards were accurate.

Then they straightened up the room and left. I hadn't made them sit a literacy or numeracy test to provide me with a baseline assessment. I hadn't let them watch film clips while I sat with each of them signing Individual Learning Plans. I hadn't done anything my contract said I should do. And I had no idea whether what I had done was useful.

But they had been engaged, they'd listened to one another, they'd all learned something, everyone had contributed and they'd left the session chatting together and in good spirits.

At the next session they all came back, on time, got the chairs out, set them in a circle and were ready to start.

Caitlin: **So who has noticed what since the last session?**

Moses: You know I go red Miss? Well yesterday, I get up in the morning blue and relaxed, then I see Dad's still drunk: ***red*** *(points to belly)*. Then I have to put dirty clothes back on cause he hasn't done laundry: ***red!*** *(Points to sternum.)* No money for bus: ***red!*** I'm cold and I'm late for school: ***red!*** *(Points to chest)*I get to school and get detention and I'm full of ***red*** right here and anyone says anything or even looks at me, it boils over! Is that why I hit people miss?

Caitlin: **I'm not sure.**

Moses: Well, if I'm already red I can walk to school past the duck pond. I can stop and look in the water, think of my Mum and breathe in blue. I could get purple before I get to school and then I won't boil so fast. Do you think that will work miss?

Caitlin: **I don't know, try it this week and let us know. What about the rest of you?**

I treated it casually but inside I was so excited. He was self-modelling. Just like one-to-one adult clients, he was finding his own answers without any real help from me. No way could I have worked out that breathing in blue by Clapton Duck Pond would be the anger management strategy that might work for this troubled teenager.

Once he had a strategy for managing his temper then they all wanted one. We set about finding the difference between one for someone who snaps and one for someone when things go quiet. These metaphor models acted as an amazing form of group learning. Each of the kids stopped being full of contempt for themselves and started getting curious about how their anger worked. They wanted to model my temper and when they discovered that when I was angry I went quiet and clipped, they playfully pointed out that they now knew they had nothing to worry about when I raised my voice.

> Each of the kids stopped being full of contempt for themselves and started getting curious about how their anger worked.

Moses was, for the first time since coming to the UK as a refugee, able to form friendships and just be a child again.

This initial modelling of tempers worked just as well for my girls' group and once we'd got the anger stuff sorted and the kids in both groups were a calmer unit, we could move on to the other themes they'd wanted to cover. Again, I went around the group with a couple of questions each until everyone had a model and had heard how differently the rest of the group did things.

Caitlin: **When you're learning at your best, you're like what?**
Kate: I'm a snail.
Caitlin: **What kind of** snail?
Kate: I'm slow but I leave a lovely silvery trail.
Caitlin: **And** slow and a lovely silvery trail. **Is there anything else about that trail?**
Kate: I can see where we've been and I can find my way from one place to another.

Caitlin: **Who's different to that?**
Naomi: I'm like a pond
Caitlin: **What kind of** pond?
Naomi: Like a pond from a fairy tale, really clear and you can see the bottom.
Caitlin: **And where does the** really clear **come from?**
Naomi: It's like a new idea gets thrown in the pond. If I look at it carefully and wait until the ripples go I can see how it fits into everything else.
Caitlin: **And for you** it's one idea thrown into a pond, **and you** leave a lovely silvery trail. **Who's different again?**

Just as with their models for anger, each kid developed and drew a metaphor map for when they were learning really well and again these went on the wall.

The Triune Brain

My overall aim was to have this form of self-modelling as the content of all the sessions and to bring in as little external theory as possible. However, there was one model I introduced to the groups early on: The Triune Brain which I'd read in Eric Jensen's *Brain-Based Teaching and Learning*. This helped me to explain the purpose of our clean modelling sessions in a simple memorable way.

The basic idea is to remember that we're animals, pure and simple. Like any animal, we need to know if we're safe from harm, well-fed and rested. We need to know whether we belong to the pack, where we fit in, what the rules are. This allows us to know where we stand and to predict what each of us might do at any one time. This knowledge allows us to develop collective trust. Only then can we free up our brains and our senses for all of the wildly creative human endeavours we're capable of.

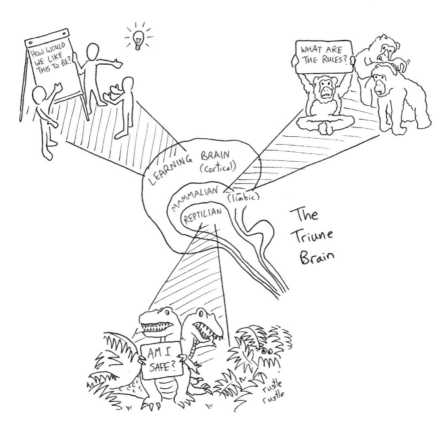

The job of the reptilian brain is to keep us alive and to put us into the state of fight, flight or freeze when we sense danger. The children were quickly able to identify when they went into this brain and make the links between whether they went into fight, like the boy who went red, or flight, like the boy with the feet that ran away. They also started to make connections between going into a reptilian state when they were trying to learn: freezing when it came to spelling, or going into 'fight' when asked to answer a question in front of the class.

The mammalian brain is all about rules, emotions and belonging to a pack. We talked about what rules or patterns they needed in order to work at their best in the sessions, we looked at the differences between their learning styles and discussed how to get shared rules that worked for all of them.

Finally, there is the neocortex or, as the group called it, the learning brain. The children could link this to their personal metaphors for learning at their best.

I was able to use this Triune Brain model to encourage them to take responsibility for keeping themselves and one another in the best state possible. I also got to share what *I* needed from the group to keep me calm and attentive. I liked the children to set up and dismantle the room and to take it in turns to go to the shops to buy fruit for snack time; this way we shared responsibility for creating our space and I felt inclined to go the extra mile for them. I found it difficult to keep the children's attention if they wandered in at different times so we started promptly at 3:45 pm. If they were late, they waited until the break to come in.

There were three groups attending the project and I so looked forward to these sessions – they were generally full of enthusiasm, happiness and laughter. Then, one afternoon, the girls seemed unusually rowdy, difficult to bring to order and were engaging in name-calling, shouting, rudeness and mayhem. I found my own voice getting uncharacteristically clipped. When we all eventually settled down, I wondered aloud what had happened to trigger this. A sullen-faced girl said, "It's you, miss. You're out of order. Kate came in late and talked over us and you didn't say nothing to her."

I had broken my own rules for the class and my behaviour triggered angry, fearful, reptilian behaviour in the girls. If the mammalian rules were to count for anything, especially in those early days when the group was just forming, those rules needed to be consistent and true. The girls wanted to see me deal effectively with Kate and when I didn't, I lost their trust and respect. This was a great lesson. I apologised, we did a Clean Set Up for how we wanted the classroom to be and they set me a Developmental Task to stick to the rules we agreed.

Modelling Maths

After 'anger' and 'learning' the kids started bringing new themes to the table. One of the biggest, surliest of the lads came in and asked quietly, before the lesson started...

Dan: Miss, don't say anything in front of them but can you do this for maths?
Caitlin: **What do you mean?**
Dan: I can't add up. I can only do baby numbers. Can you use this to make your brain add up like a calculator?
Caitlin: **Let's try it.**

Caitlin: **OK guys, we're going to model maths today.**
Kile: What for miss?
Talib: I hate maths.
Arfin: Oh no miss, I can't add up!
Caitlin: **I said we're going to model maths not do maths. Just add 2 and 3. Don't tell me the answer. When you're adding 2 and 3, what happens?**
Kile: I see the 2 and 3 in front of me then an equal sign and then the 5.
Caitlin: **Anything else about the 2, 3 and 5?**
Kile: They're black on a white background.
Dan: In mine, I've got two dots and three dots and they get together and then the answer comes up.
Caitlin: **And** the answer comes up, **what happens just before** the answer comes up?
Dan: It's like they get into a lift together and 5 comes out at the next floor.
Caitlin: **OK, who's different again?**
Talib: I don't do that! I feel it in my fingers.
Caitlin: **Whereabouts** in your fingers?

Talib: In the tips, like I'm counting on them.

Caitlin: **Great, now add 5 plus 7.**

Kile: That's the same miss, written up like sums on the board.

Caitlin: **Who's different?**

Talib: It's still my fingers miss, but I run out and they get muddled.

Caitlin: **And is there anything else about those** fingers?

Talib: They feel clumsy.

Caitlin: **Who's different again?**

Dan: Oh that's too heavy for my lift.

Caitlin: **And when it's** too heavy, **then what happens?**

Dan: It needs oil.

Caitlin: **What kind of** oil?

Dan: No, it's OK, I've got it … 5 and 7 make 12.

Caitlin: **What happens just before** you've got it?

Dan: I don't know but the answer comes up when there's oil.

It was an extraordinary experience: the children modelled themselves, shared ideas and updated their models with hardly any leading, tugging or pushing. I had very little idea of what I was up to or of why it was working but it was certainly keeping the kids interested. The children developed their individual models for reading, spelling, times tables, addition, the past and the future, setting goals and getting into a good state.

I was developing a stronger sense of what I was classifying as contempt and what I meant by moving to curiosity. Contempt meant thinking that a reaction, an attitude, a person or a group of people were unacceptable as they were.

Curiosity meant noticing how things were and wondering how they've come to be like this and what we might like to have happen next. This application of David Grove's work, at a group level, was creating a culture of curiosity that moved the whole group out of contempt and meant deep learning was taking place for all of us.

Hidden Contempt

There were occasions when I still made huge mistakes. Generally these were times when I took the position of expert instead of modeller and decided that what the children were doing needed my intervention to change things.

One young man, James, was clearly very, very clever, but almost completely illiterate. When the children were teaching each other visual spelling techniques they noticed that James could learn a word one minute and read all of the letters forwards and backwards, then he wouldn't recognise it written down a few moments later. One of the boys spotted what was happening by watching James point to the letters he was seeing in his mind in a vertical line.

Moses: Miss, when James is learning the word and spelling it out, he's not seeing it sideways 'because', he's seeing it up and down.

James: Oh that's because I only have a little bit of space to put the letters in.

And he showed us a thin bit of space in front of him, only wide enough for single letters. The boys were immediately very eager to help and offered to write out stories vertically so that James could read them the way he saw them in his mind. Instead of remaining in a facilitative role, a naive expert on James' learning, I leaned over to him and said, "This vertical space you have for seeing letters, I just need you to open it up and make it …"

James kicked over the table and stormed out. We sat in stunned silence and waited but he was gone.

It was three weeks before he came back and I asked him for a one-to-one session to find out what had happened:

James: You shamed me in front of everyone miss.

Caitlin: **I know I did something wrong. Can you help me understand what?**

James: I can't open up that space.

Caitlin: **When** you can't open up that space, **does** that space **have a size or a shape?**

James: It's wavy.

Caitlin: **What kind of** wavy?

James: Like curtains.

Caitlin: **And** wavy, like curtains … **is there anything else?**

James: They're curtains I hide behind.

Caitlin: **What kind of** I **is that?**

James: I'm six.

Caitlin: **And what kind of** hide **is the** hide behind those curtains?

James: My dad's home and he's beating my mum and I'm hiding so he doesn't get me, but I need to watch and see if I have to run and get an ambulance for my mum.

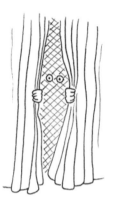

It was so clear how thoughtless I'd been. Instead of wondering what would have to be true for him to have only a bit of vertical space to keep his letters in, I'd decided it needed to change. I didn't have a therapeutic contract to work one-to-one with these kids so I couldn't offer James a full clean modelling session, in which he might have been able to transform his system and regain full access to his visual thinking. Instead I needed to work with what was there:

Caitlin: **James, when you only have this** wavy space **to think in, AND in order to learn to read you need to store words horizontally, what needs to happen now?**

James: I could write them very small and very close up.

Caitlin: **And can you** write them small and close up?

James: They keep moving.

Caitlin: **And what needs to happen when** they keep moving?
James: I need to chisel them onto stone.
Caitlin: **And can you** chisel them onto stone?
James: Yes.

In the next lesson, slowly and carefully, he lifted his hands and chiselled 'because' in tiny letters in the air in front of him. Later on in that lesson, he could pick the word correctly out of a sentence. And slowly and painstakingly James learned to read a few words a week, chiselling them into his stone. Gradually he didn't have to consciously chisel each word but was able to learn them unconsciously. The literacy that had eluded him for so long was now something he could access again.

I'm sorry that he had to suffer for my learning but it was a deep lesson in why you should stay curious about things you don't understand rather than wading in and deciding how they should change.

> It was a deep lesson in why you should stay curious about things you don't understand rather than wading in and deciding how they should change.

I realised how important it was that I'd started from a position of not knowing. If I'd started the sessions by asking Moses to control his temper or James to learn to read, then I would have given them the message that they weren't good enough as they were. It's true that a part of Moses wanted to be able to control his temper, but part of him wanted to scream and shout and hit things. It's true that part of James wanted to learn to read, but part of him was so caught up in early trauma that he didn't have access to his visual memory.

By starting from a position of acceptance, the message was that everybody was OK, their stuff was OK, all the different aspects of their psyches were OK, right there, right now, in that moment.

Clean modelling created space for them to gather all the parts of themselves together, map them out and work out what they were there for. David Grove used to say that once we paid due diligence to all of the various parts of our clients, those parts could confess their strengths and be released from their roles. This would then enable clients to reorganise their experience

> Once we pay due diligence to all of the various parts of our clients, those parts can confess their strengths and be released from their roles.

and their responses to it, which allow them to manifest new behaviours and new experiences in the world. Something like that was happening here, at a group level rather than within an individual system. The results meant that the kids weren't just updating their own life stories and changing their own patterns, they were watching and listening to one another do it too. They were hearing all kinds of stories that were outside of their experience and were becoming wise and articulate in ways I hadn't imagined.

Moses had joined the group while feeling full of shame and loneliness. Now he could recognise his red temper as fear of the fighting he'd witnessed first-hand in Sierra Leone; the injustice of being forced to flee the country with a father he didn't know well; the grief of leaving his beloved mother behind to an uncertain fate; the loss of the helpful, hopeful boy he used to be. By honouring all parts of his system through non-judgemental modelling he could re-access his capability both to calm himself down and to name what was happening to him.

When a Group Begins to Self-Model

Even though we were having a great time together, this was a nine-month project and I didn't want the children to become too strongly attached to me and then be upset when the project came to an end. I wanted them to develop the skills to build relationships, with one another and with other safe adults, that would support them long after the project was finished.

Penny and James, within their Symbolic Modelling process, used the term self-modelling to describe what their clients were doing. The facilitator was there to keep the process on track but the client was taking over the modelling process. In a similar way, I didn't want to be responsible for being the clean modeller in these groups; I was hoping they'd learn the clean questions and the modelling processes and start to take the reins themselves.

Initially, I had led the group and used the clean questions to help the children build up their metaphor models. I offered them Clean Feedback and I used the Clean Set Up to help them think about their own outcomes. I encouraged them to use Developmental Tasks to get more flexibility or to try one another's learning strategies. Then, over a few weeks, as their personal patterns were uncovered and they were able to celebrate their own and each other's strengths, their attention began to move from contempt to curiosity. They wanted to know how things worked and what could be done about them. They started using the tools outside of the sessions. One boy explained to his teachers that he couldn't manage crowds in the corridor and they agreed he could arrive at the class early and leave early so he could keep his state calmer. One girl shared that her teacher had said that her form group would never amount to anything and she'd asked "What's your evidence for that miss?" I'm not sure these changes were always welcomed by other adults but I felt that the children now had some tools to ask for what they needed and to work out when other people were being unfair.

There was a lovely point in my work with the girls' group when I was rattling off instructions to the class and Mary Lou interrupted me.

Mary Lou: You've got to slow down, miss. You're talking too fast.
Caitlin: **What do you mean Mary Lou? You talk faster than me.**
Mary Lou: It's not for me, it's for Naomi. When she's learning at her best she likes to get one idea like a pebble in a pond and then the ripples to settle, so she knows she's got it. When you talk fast it's like you're throwing pebbles at her and she's all over the place.

She was absolutely right and I needed to be told. The kids had moved from learners to facilitators and were now starting to advocate for one another's needs.

Tony Blair, when he was the UK Prime Minister, visited our project and James showed how his new spelling and reading strategies were working and Moses shared how the temper metaphor helped him keep his cool. There was a comment from one of the visitors that these kids were clearly staged for the PM and couldn't be the 'really bad' ones. That was a compliment on the kids' new-found communication skills but a damning indictment on the politician's belief in the potential of teenagers to change and grow.

These children were the greatest of teachers, sharp and observant and with no tolerance for inconsistency. In so many ways they co-created the foundation for the approach in this book that would later be called Systemic Modelling™.

Cautionary Tale

This was a fantastic first example of what was possible when the work of David Grove was applied to groups. Sixty per cent of the young people were back in mainstream education by the end of the nine months and the project won a European Community Safety award for our work.

I'm sharing the next part of this story not to suggest that the way these groups were run wasn't worth doing – it was – but to highlight that these kinds of changes need to be supported in the wider system if they are to become sustainable.

If you think back to the start of this story, you'll recall that the mainstream education system that these children were re-entering was far from safe.

Moses, who used to be in a constant state of 'red' was now a much calmer happier child, very positive and a lot of fun. The other children knew he didn't have enough to eat at home and that he was often hungry. About seven months into the project, while in the dinner hall at school, something happened to change the course of his life again:

Dan: Oh, I haven't touched my pasty, would you like it?
Moses: Sure.
Dan: I'll just go and get you a fork.

Dan went off to get a fork and Moses slid the food tray with the pasty over in front of him. A dinner lady came behind him, grabbed his arm, and said:

DL: Don't steal his food.
Moses: He said I could have it.
DL: Don't lie to me.
Moses: Get off me, I'm not lying.
DL: Right you're going to the teacher.

And she dragged him across the dining hall to the teacher in charge, and told him that Moses had been stealing food and was lying about it.

The other children were crowding round trying to explain that she was wrong but no one would listen to them. Moses was protesting his innocence but the teacher shouted him down. The dinner lady said that everyone knew Moses was a liar and a thief. Then Moses hit her and was immediately expelled from school.

No one asked what had led up to him suddenly hitting someone after six months of good behaviour. He wasn't allowed space to explain what had happened or to try to make amends. The other children had no opportunity to explain their side of the story. He was taken off our programme and not allowed to attend any more of the sessions. Even my own boss said, "Well we've got to be seen to support the school rules, if he's not going to be part of the school we can't deal with him anymore." And he was gone, just like that.

In that moment I felt that I'd done Moses a massive disservice by supporting him to build relationships and then releasing him into a system where the people in charge weren't going through the same level of personal development as the young people.

I wanted my next project to be one in which the leaders of the system were as interested in changing themselves as they were in getting other people to change. I looked around for a wider change programme in education and youth work but instead found one in the business sector.

CHAPTER 3

Metaphors at Work

*Developing a shared corporate metaphor
for a software development company
working at its best*

I received a call from a director of a company that creates collaborative software solutions, who said, "I really like the strapline you use to describe your work on your website: *We train exquisite attention on individual systems and systems of individuals.* Can you do this work with a business team?

This hadn't been what I was expecting. I was very much a scruffy youth worker with no experience of the corporate world.

Caitlin: **I'm not sure … What would you like to have happen?**

Chris: We've got programmers who create software we aren't able to market and marketers who won't even talk to the programmers and a leverage team in the middle acting like permanent mediators. I want a more unified company, with a sense of common purpose and a shared set of values at our core.

That sounded more like something that I could tackle and helping to resolve conflict like this was certainly in line with my compelling path. I was just a bit nervous about whether I had anything valuable to offer. I said, "The process might be able to do that but it hasn't been used in business before. How about I spend some more time with you and the other director in the company. I'll use clean modelling to clarify the current behaviours in your team and get really clear about what it is you both want to have happen next. This gives the two of you a chance to test the process before we take it to your team. And it gives me a chance to find out if I've anything useful to offer. I won't charge you for this session but if it's useful, the three of us will come away with a shared model for what I'm helping you to achieve and the behaviours that will let you know the project is working."

He agreed, and I met up with Chris and his co-director Robert at the Institute of Directors in London dressed in a business suit I'd borrowed from my mother and hoping I looked the part.

I conducted the meeting like a modelling session using the Karma Cycle: Clean Feedback on what was already happening in their team; Clean Set Up to discover (a) what they wanted to have happen, (b) their part in the process and (c) what they needed and expected from me; and Developmental Tasks to move their attention towards action.

Caitlin: **When you have this** shared model**, then what happens?**
Robert: I'll know we have a shared set of core values and I'll trust we'll make similar decisions.
Caitlin: **What will you be seeing and hearing that will let you know the team** has a shared set of core values?
Robert: They would collaborate on new products and share programming and market information enthusiastically together.

Although I'd asked for what he'd see and hear, Robert had replied with a higher level description. I simply accepted his answer and asked another evidence based question.

Caitlin: **And as** they collaborate on new products **what will you be seeing and hearing when** they're sharing information enthusiastically?
Robert: They'll be walking across the office, spending time in each other's company.

Just as with Clean Feedback, I was helping him to clarify his outcome in terms of evidence, inference and impact – what would he be seeing and hearing when he had what he wanted, what would this mean for him and what did he hope would be the impact on the team and on their business.

I then asked about current practice, again separating his answers into what he'd seen and heard, what he was making up and what difference that made to the business.

Caitlin: **What are things like at the moment?**
Chris: Oh, the programmers have their own area of the office and the
          marketers never go there unless they have to.
Caitlin: **When** the marketers never go to the programmers area, **then what
          happens?**
Chris: We end up with waste or miscommunication because it's all done by
          email and there's not enough clarification.

As I asked these questions, I was wondering: What could be the value of this?
Are they projecting onto each other's behaviour? What would they like to have
happen?

Again I noticed when the director was talking about things they'd actually seen
and heard and when they were talking about things they were 'making up' – i.e.
where they were making assumptions without any actual evidence. I was also
noticing whether the things they were making up were full of contempt or full of
curiosity; this helped me gauge their attitude to the team as it stood.

I thought they might think I was a bit crazy asking all of these odd questions
and I had no idea whether business people already knew this kind of information.
But it seemed to go OK and Chris and Robert began to notice what kinds
of things they were making up about their team. They noticed patterns in
themselves and things they might have to do differently. The process seemed to
help them to articulate their outcomes in more depth and to ensure that they
were aligned.

This was an extension of what Dee and I had developed together to unpack our
own conflict or create shared outcomes and I was thrilled to discover that these
two business directors were finding it useful too.

While I was building the two models, the difference between what they knew was actually happening and what they wanted to have happen took shape and I could feel the structure of what needed to happen next and a clean intervention emerged between the two models.

'Metaphors at Work' Emerges

This was the first full piece of 'Clean Scoping' I'd ever done but I was so immersed in the process I forgot that I was new to business and didn't know what I was talking about. All of my attention was on the model of the issues and outcomes we'd built during the meeting and as that model became clear so did the clean intervention. The words seemed to tumble out one after another as I described what needed to happen, almost as a fait accompli. I've laid it out in detail here because although it was the first attempt at a clean business process, the structure has stood the test of time and has been used in every kind of context since.

"I think this could work as a four-stage, iterative process so that people have a go with the metaphors, then another go, and another, with each stage building on the one before – until by the end it's second nature.

"The **first stage** could be a one-to-one modelling session with each member of the team, getting five individual models for: when *they're* working at their best; an *ideal team* that supports them to work at their best; when their *department* is at it's best; what the *organisation* is *currently* like; and what the organisation *would need to be like* in order for them to work at their best more of the time.

"Let's start one-to-one because people can't always articulate their personal patterns to themselves, never mind in public. They'll need space to explore and reflect on their internal metaphors.

"The **second stage** will be in departmental groups. I'll use an exercise I've developed called 'Five Senses' where people explore how they make sense of what someone is saying to them. It's really simple. Starting with 'seeing', I'll say, "See an elephant" and they'll all imagine an elephant and then I'll ask what kind of elephant it is, where it is, does it have a size and so on. Then I'll ask about the other four senses, with instructions such as, "Hear music", "Taste a lemon", "Feel velvet" and "Smell smoke." This will help them see how different their internal models are from one another and how quickly they jump to conclusions. It's a mini version of what we'll do with their metaphor models later.

"After this exercise they'll be ready to share their individual metaphors for working at their best with their team mates and to use these metaphors to understand where each of them is coming from. Using the Five Senses I'll teach them not to jump too quickly to interpreting what each metaphor means. Next they can share their metaphors for an ideal team and they can ask questions, both clean and 'dirty' to build up group intelligence about the similarities and differences between them. They can practise the clean questions with people they know well and already work effectively with.

"Each departmental group can then develop a shared metaphor for when their team is working at its best. This will let them negotiate their individual needs and create a joint model that allows all of them to work at their best more of the time. A bit like I just did with you two to get you to a shared model for this project. They can test whether this joint model has an immediate positive benefit on how they work together.

"In **stage three**, all three departments will come together to share their departmental metaphors. I'll probably get them in threes to share their individual metaphors as a warm up. Then each department can share their departmental metaphors, ask cleanish questions to clarify what's important to each departmental team and think about what's been working well and not so well.

"Once we're clear on the departments, the whole team can share their individual metaphors

for the organisation at its best and develop a joint company metaphor that they can all sign up to.

"In **stage four**, we'll take some live issues and practise using the joint metaphor and the clean modelling tools to resolve them."

I stopped and looked at the two directors. What would they think of all that? I was suddenly feeling like I'd be found out and they'd realise that I was making it all up and send me packing. But they thought this sounded like a great plan and were eager to go ahead. I was a little bit cautious, especially after the recent expulsion of Moses at the youth project and started checking for their ability to cope with all of the unknowns that come with a project like this:

Caitlin: **What if I ask the individuals what they need to work at their best and they want the two of you to change fundamentally?"**

Chris: Then we'll need to re-look at our practice or at our team because that will be useful information.

Caitlin: **What if I model a department and as they develop their shared model, it completely clashes with your values?**

Robert: That will be information too. I won't develop a company where I don't believe in the core values but I would value knowing if the majority of the people I'd hired had different values to me.

Caitlin: **What if I model an individual and as they get more in touch with their values, they decide they want to do something else?**

Chris: I'd much rather people were doing what they really wanted to do. An employee whose heart isn't in it can cause a lot of difficulties and they usually leave after creating a lot of strife. If this process accelerates that process, that would be great.

They made all the right noises so I felt confident that we could all be open to whatever emerged.

Looking back, I was very, very lucky that my first foray into business was with two pioneering leaders in creating collaborative learning organisations. It could so easily have ended in humiliation or incredulity. We followed the process almost exactly as I had laid it out in that first meeting – and in subsequent projects I've often found that if I scope cleanly and deeply in the first session, the model that emerges is usually a good fit.

Serendipity

John Martin was an academic from the Systems Department of the UK Open
University, an institution dedicated to academic excellence for those who need
to study at a distance and he serendipitously enters the tale here. Throughout the
1980s he had been involved in teaching creative thinking to civil servants, and
in the early '90s this had morphed into a very popular 'Creative Management'
course as part of the new Business School's MBA.

The residential version of this course already included small-scale
demonstrations of problem solving entirely at the level of imagery and metaphor,
but they were dependent on the presence of a skilled facilitator. For the students
who attended these demonstrations, a door into another world was often opened,
but they didn't get the skills to go through the door and do this work themselves.

John had a vague idea of needing to find simple, non-scary, robust, easily
taught, processes that would work for everyone – the 'hard-boiled' as well as the
'touchy-feely'. It had seemed a very tall order. Penny and James had suggested
he might benefit from talking to me and when I told him about the software
company project I was working on, it sounded as if this could be exactly what he
was looking for. With the directors' agreement, a BBC film crew came in with
their cameras and captured the process as we went along. Although it seemed as
if there was going to be a lot of attention on my first piece of work in business,
it also meant that this innovative development in Clean Language would be
recorded in a way that would make it accessible to others after the project.

Getting Over the First 'Metaphors at Work' Hurdle

I arrived at the office, my first experience in a corporate environment, a little
nervous with no idea what to expect. A man introduced himself as Tom and said,
"Chris tells me that my participation on this metaphor project is voluntary. I'm
already too busy; tell me why I should spend six days of my precious time doing
this. You can have five minutes."

Tom was in charge of the IT infrastructure and I knew, from the model I'd
made of the company during the Clean Scoping, that he was a key person in this
project. He interacted with everyone else in the team and was highly influential.
If he wasn't on board, the whole thing might fall apart. I flustered for a minute
and then settled into a modelling frame of mind, telling myself:

- I am a pattern detector.
- I am not trying to get anyone to change their mindset.
- I am simply paying exquisite attention to them.
- I'll be feeding information back to them and only sharing my own thinking when necessary.
- I need to trust that Tom and I will both will benefit from this quality of attention.

Caitlin: **Rather than me tell you about it, how about we do it for the five minutes and you can see if it's useful or not?**

He agreed and we took a seat.

Caitlin: **If this project to create a company metaphor were to be really useful for you, it will be like what?**

Tom: I have no idea what you mean. I don't do metaphors.

Caitlin: **OK. Well if this project were perfect for me it would be like going white water rafting. We'd all get into the raft with minimal idea about where we're going or how we'll work as a team. We start off in shallow, gentle waters but as we get a feel for the group and the river we can take on exhilarating stretches of rapids with confidence. I can imagine us leaning right out of the raft at times - even falling in and being able to get to shore and start again.**

Tom: *(Leaning away from me with cold eyes.)* That's enough; I can see that I wouldn't want to work with you. I'd hate this.

Caitlin: **OK, so if you know** you'd hate this, **and we've still got four minutes, what would an ideal project be like for you?**

Tom: It would be more like designing the blueprints for a building.

Caitlin: **What kind of** blueprints?

Tom: The blueprints would be just the right dimensions and all of the details would be to scale. They are things of beauty in their own right, even before the building is made.

Caitlin: **Is there anything else about the** designing **of those** blueprints?

Tom: I'd be carefully drawing up the plans, figuring out how to assemble the right building team, and then start building a structure that will look good from every angle. Everyone knows what to expect at each stage and I know the right people will be doing the right things at the right time.

I felt my shoulders tightening as if I had a straitjacket on. I could feel why my metaphors wouldn't resonate with him.

Caitlin: **OK, suppose this project was compulsory, what would have to change in my metaphor for you to be able to work well with me?**

Tom: There would need to be some purpose for the trip at the beginning. Then I'd want maps to see where we are and times we can stop along the way and check we're on the right track. I'd need something to do along the way such as mapping or collecting samples from the new territory we're rafting down.

Caitlin: **That would be fine for me. We'll need to start with a clear outcome for the project and we will need someone to record what we find in a meaningful way. This is an experiment but if it is successful it needs to be replicable. With your metaphor of** blue prints**, would it be possible to have them done in pencil so that they can be adjusted as the** building **takes shape?"**

Tom: Fine with me, so long as the adjustments are also things of beauty and done with care and attention to detail… OK I get it. If we hadn't done this you would just irritate me and I wouldn't know why, I'd just avoid or badmouth you. These metaphors are for understanding each other and working out how to get the best from each other. I'm in.

Phew! Once Tom was on board, metaphorically, then everyone else engaged with it and we could begin.

Stage 1: Individual Interviews

My first task was to interview each member of the team privately and I was careful to start off conversationally and pace how comfortable they were answering clean questions. With some we were straight into full-blown metaphors:

- I'm like a whirling dervish.
- An ideal team is a skein of geese, taking it in turns to be the leader.
- This company is like a laboratory full of rats.

But with others the answers would be much more cognitive:

- I'm organised and clear about my goal.
- An ideal team is committed.
- This company is non-hierarchical.

In these cases I learned that if you keep asking for metaphors people disengage really quickly. Instead I had to keep asking clean questions quite conversationally to tease out the structure of their thinking.

Caitlin: **What kind of** organised?
Paul: Everything is lined up with a clear boundary.
Caitlin: **And** organised **and** clear about your goal, **and is there anything else about** clear?
Paul: There are milestones as well as an end result.
Caitlin: **And whereabouts could those** milestones **be?**
Paul: Evenly spaced *(gestures with hand in front of him)*.

After each interview I asked people to make maps of their metaphors to help share their ideas with colleagues. I'd done this with the children too, asked them to draw their metaphor as a way of making it memorable to their colleagues. There were a few quips about being back in primary school but everyone engaged in it and there was a lot of concentration and eagerness to look at each others drawings.

Stage 2: Departmental Group

Next I brought the individuals together in their departmental teams, with their maps and their metaphors, got them into a circle and explained that I was going to run an exercise to help them to find out how differently each of them structured their thinking. I used the metaphor of uncovering their unconscious architecture so that it matched the kind of language software people understood.

This was going to be a concentrated version of an exercise we'd done in the practice group and with the youth project. Instead of taking a theme and exploring it in depth, I would give them simple instructions such as "See an elephant", "Listen to music" or "Feel ice" and then ask them each two or three clean questions each to help them compare their own thinking with one another's. We started with visualising.

Caitlin: **See an elephant.** *(Pause for whole group to process their answers.)* **What kind of elephant is it?**
Robert: Large and grey
Caitlin: **And it's** large and grey – **and whereabouts is that elephant?**
Robert: By a watering hole, with a baby elephant next to it.
Caitlin: **Is there anything else about that** baby elephant?
Robert: Shy, hiding behind his mother's legs.

With each question, Robert was sharing more detail about his first thought. At the same time, the rest of the group were listening to his answers and making their own images of what they thought Robert was seeing. Whenever the answer wasn't what they expected they would have to update their personal model of Robert's elephant. Every now and then, I stopped the exercise and asked the group what was happening as they got new information about someone's image.

Simon: I really like it. I can imagine the baby and the rest of the family.

Caitlin: **Who's different to that?**

Richard: I hear what he says but I just prefer the one I've imagined so I ignore him.

Chris: I had to move the baby I imagined from in front of its mother to hiding behind her.

From seeing elephants we went onto hearing music, smelling smoke, feeling ice and tasting lemon. This exercise gave me a chance to show them WHY they should ask clean questions and how quickly and easily they made assumptions about what people meant. I would refer to this exercise later on when they were sharing their models for working at their best and their ideal team. It's a simple way to introduce the idea that some people find it easier to process certain senses than others. This way people aren't surprised when some have visual metaphors and others are all about feelings.

From here we went smoothly into sharing their individual metaphors for working at their best:

Dan: When I'm working at my best I'm like a busy bee flying from flower to flower gathering nectar but then I need a big sit down to release the weight of all that nectar before I can start flying around again.

I opened this up to the small group and they asked questions to develop the metaphor, to understand how this person worked and how they could support them. If someone asked a cleanish question such as, "What are the flowers in your metaphor?" Dan would answer. But if someone asked a leading or 'dirty' question such as, "If you're flying from flower to flower, then won't you leave projects half-finished?" I would ask that person a couple of questions to uncover the assumptions they were making:

Caitlin: **What happens to you when he says he** flies from flower to flower?
Tom: Oh I'm worried that he's doing a bit of this and a bit of that and that deadlines won't be hit. I'm imagining him flitting around at work and I won't know where I am.
Caitlin: **When that is what** you're imagining **might happen, what's a cleanish question you could ask to find out what happens for the** bee?

Tom then had another go at asking a clean question:

Tom: **When** you're flying from flower to flower, **what happens with work projects?**

Dan: Oh I do little bits here and there, and each project helps me think about the other projects. But like the waggle dance bees do, I can remember clearly where I've been and where I still have to go. After my rest, I digest what I've learned and go and finish getting all the nectar from the flowers.

In this spirit of non-judgemental inquiry, the group started to notice the difference between when their questions were unclean and when they were clean. Unclean was when they were asking questions that came out of their own model and clean when their questions were based on the other person's model. Over the sessions most people got cleaner and cleaner and when they did ask a 'dirty' question, they would catch themselves doing it and start laughing.

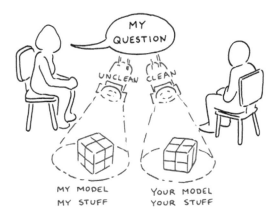

The next stage was for them to share their metaphors for an ideal team and the rules and support they needed to keep their mammalian brains happy.

As each person shared their team metaphor for how they liked to work in a group, I actively encouraged the others to ask for evidence of what they'd see or hear, like this:

Dan: An ideal team for me is completely committed.

Robert: **When they're** committed, **that's** committed **like what?**

Dan: Like a group of skiers.

Robert: **Is there anything else about those** skiers?

Dan: At the start of the day we talk about where we're likely to ski and who'll be doing what. Then people go off and do their own thing but they keep within what they agreed. If anyone wants to go off-piste they let at least a couple of people know for safety reasons. It's loose but it's also a really safe structure.

Robert: **And what would I see and hear in this office when** we're committed like skiers? *(Evidence-based question.)*

Dan: Since none of us are great at using the Intranet, we'd have a brief morning meeting, everyone there, on time but informal. Who's working on what projects today and who is flitting between projects, like my bee? A quick check-in but if anyone goes off to see a client or changes their plans they tell a couple of other people so that the rest of us can adjust our plans too.

The group were able to switch between metaphors and reality and back again with increasing ease and could use both kinds of information to increase their understanding. This seemed very much like my idea of navigating the rapids in our white water raft and I was so excited.

Some people got the idea straight away and asked cleanish questions to gather information. Others wouldn't get it at all and would exasperate the group:

Robert: When I'm working at my best, I'm like a tall tree that can bend in the wind.

Rick: Like an oak? *(Dirty question.)*

Robert: No not an oak, more like…

Rick: But oaks are tall and flexible, that's why they live so long. *(Interrupting with dirty comment.)*

Robert: Well I was thinking more of a sapling.

Rick: It could be an oak sapling. *(Dirty comment.)*

When this happened I stepped in and asked the interrupter a couple of questions about the oak that they were focussed on:

Caitlin: **What kind of** oak **is your** oak?

Rick: It's tall and strong rooted.

Caitlin: **And where is your** oak?

Rick: It's here in my feet and chest.

Caitlin: **And your** oak **is** tall and strong rooted **and** here in your feet and chest *(points to him)* **and keeping your** oak **here** *(keeps on pointing)*, **ask a few of these cleanish questions to find out about his sapling** *(points to Robert)* **and notice the differences between the two.**

Even if Rick never quite got it, the rest of the group had a structure for what he was doing when he mixed up what they'd said with what he was thinking. The clean questions helped to illustrate clearly where his attention was in the interaction. I needed to be there on behalf of Rick as well as on behalf of the group because the way he was behaving was indicative of the way lots of people behave and I wanted the group to develop strategies for still treating him respectfully, while also making their communication clearer.

Once they'd shared their ideal team metaphors, it was time to develop a shared departmental metaphor – one that they could all sign up to. I asked them to consider:

Caitlin: **What could be a model or metaphor that encapsulates all of the things that are most important to you as individuals in a team?**

After that I left them to their own devices, only intervening if someone wasn't paying attention to the assumptions in their questions or if I hadn't heard from someone in the group for a while.

I might ask questions as a way of advocating on behalf of the other people's metaphors. For example, if the group were all talking about being on the same page and I was aware that one of them valued diversity as key to a high functioning team, I would ask, "So where is the diversity in this model?" But this was rare; people seem to grasp the methodology very quickly and would refer back to the individual metaphors for reference.

Once the group had a joint metaphor I asked them to map it out and to check they all agreed with it.

Stage 3: Getting a Joint Company Metaphor

So now we had three separate departments, each with their own departmental metaphor and it was time for the whole company, of 12 people, to come together. By this time, at least two-thirds of the group were adept at asking and answering clean questions and at separating out what was presented from what people were inferring. People were listening well, building on, or clarifying, what was said and making great connections across the group. It was a pleasure to watch. They took pens to the white board, sketched out ideas, updated them and took turns drawing possibilities. They were remarkably outcome focussed and moved swiftly from possible conflicts to solutions that suited both parties. They were advocating for ideas that weren't their own which indicated to me that they were thinking on a group level rather than fighting their own corners.

The metaphor that emerged from these discussions was a part-mechanical dolphin with a hidden research centre – beautiful, friendly and approachable but with power beyond people's expectations. Once the metaphor started to emerge the team focussed around it and checked that it had all of the aspects that were important to each them. One of the more artistic members of the team drew it and it went up on the wall. I left them to get used to it.

One of the things I really wanted to know was, "So what?". What difference had developing these joint metaphors actually made? I asked for a short break in the project to reflect on what had happened and to evaluate the impact before we moved on. The results were both surprising and encouraging. Although the attention had simply been on developing and sharing individual metaphors and taking on some very simple tools for clarifying what someone meant when they spoke, the team reported that they were now having a consistently different experience with one another:

- We have shorter and more productive meetings.
- We get less emotional when we're discussing conflicting ideas.
- It's like the metaphors put a distance between the ideas and each of us – we're both talking about an idea, not criticising one another.
- Clean questions are like a Dyno-Rod® through our communication channels.
- I've now lost confidence that I've ever understood anything that anyone has said to me. And that's great.
- When we make a decision now it sticks, we don't have to go over it again.

As well as a joint company metaphor, this software company now had a group of individuals who understood themselves and one another much better – and there were lots of knock-on effects of this change. Even though we hadn't put any direct attention on this outcome, the marketers and the programmers began to meet for coffee and wander into one another's office spaces. All of the evidence for success that Robert, Chris and I had built into the initial proposal was being demonstrated.

Stage 4: Live Applications

I still had some days for putting the clean modelling into practice on live issues. This was to ensure that the group would have the skills to use the tools for generating new ideas after I'd left. So I asked Robert and Chris what they'd like to have happen next. There were a few issues they thought this approach might be able to help with and we chose one as a starting point.

Modelling Creativity and Productivity

The first issue related to a conflict between the directors and one of their employees. Rupert, who'd recently been recruited as a programmer, had seemed amazingly creative but he wasn't performing very well. The two directors wanted to work out what was happening and whether they could manage him differently.

Caitlin: **Currently what's happening?**
Chris: Rupert's not performing. He often seems quite distracted and we find he's doing things unrelated to work. He misses lots of deadlines and needs reminding but then still doesn't produce anything.

Caitlin: **What are you currently doing with him?**

Chris: We're giving him tighter deadlines and making sure there are fewer projects on his radar. We take it in turns to try keeping him on task so he's more productive.

Caitlin: **What would you like to have happen with Rupert?**

Chris: We'd like him to be at his most creative - the reason we hired him. We'd like him to be contributing to the business with innovative solutions in a timely way. We'd also like to be managing him more effectively and helping to get the most from him.

I brought Rupert and the directors together. The directors shared their outcomes for wanting to find out more about Rupert's thinking process and he agreed to take part in the session. I started by asking him how he worked at his best and then used clean questions to expand his answers into a metaphor landscape.

Caitlin: **When you're working at your best, you're like what?**

Rupert: I'm creative.

Caitlin: **That's** creative **like what?**

Rupert: It's like there's a sudden spark *(snaps his finger from behind his head forward in front of him)*.

Caitlin: **And where does that** spark **come from?**

Rupert: From behind me – it's like a primordial soup.

Caitlin: **And when there's a** spark **that comes from** behind you, a primordial soup, **then what happens?**

Rupert: *(Snaps his finger again and points his finger in front of him.)* It flies to its landing site.

Caitlin: **What kind of** landing site?

Rupert: They're things I'm working on, they're out in front of me, flashing.

Caitlin: **And how many** landing sites are there?

Rupert: About seven

Caitlin: **And what happens just before** a spark flies **like that?**

Rupert: If I try and make it happen the spark never comes. I need to be looking the other way for the primordial soup to send out a spark. Maybe reading New Scientist or browsing biological viruses or playing a new Internet game. Everything I'm learning feeds this primordial soup, gets mixed in. All of the different ideas and structures just keep feeding it.

Rupert: When I'm not
looking that's when
the spark will come.
It, kind of, flies out
of the primordial
soup and lands on the
relevant site as a fully
formed solution.

His bosses quickly understood
how his creativity worked and
realised that by reducing the
number of projects he was working on, there were fewer landing sites and fewer
opportunities for sparks to fly. Similarly by focusing him on specific projects and
reminding him of deadlines, they disrupted the crucial 'looking the other way'
part of his process.

It was clear to all three parties that the way that the directors were trying to
manage Rupert was completely at odds with his metaphor and that if they kept
on doing it he'd be unable to perform. Either he could try to change or they
could.

After the 20-minute clean modelling session they decided to give him nine
projects to be thinking about concurrently, ensuring all his landing sites could
be covered with work-based projects. They dropped the deadlines to see whether
they were more likely to be hit if he was 'looking the other way'. He became
more of a roving innovator and his productivity went up immediately. When
I followed up with them, three years later, they were all still happy with this
arrangement and he was highly productive within the company.

Metaphor For a New Product

The company also wanted to try using clean questions to get a better
understanding of the products they were developing. Simon was leading the
development of a fantastic new product – Electronic Laboratory Notebooks –
and he wanted to think through ways to explain them to customers. He asked
for a session to help him crystallise his thinking. This time the group led the
modelling rather than me.

Simon:	It needs to have a consistent internal structure but different faces so that different aspects can be highlighted for different areas of our customer's business.
Tom:	**And when it will** have different faces, **how many** different faces?
Simon:	I'm not sure. At least five, maybe more. For example, the scientists are going to want to see one facet of the product – and they'll ask, "How does this save me time and help me find things?" The lawyers are generally only going to be concerned about Patent Evidence, so we'll need a different façade for them to view the product through. Then there'll be management, there'll be IT… the list goes on.
Robert:	**And** the list goes on, and different facets, and consistent internal structure. **Is there anything else about** consistent internal structure?
Simon:	When they do speak together about the product, it's important that the way we describe it is consistent and has the same kind of feel so they don't feel we're duping them. *(Uses hands to show multiple planes that the product could be viewed through.)*
Tom:	**And when** it's consistent and has different faces, **it's like what?**
Simon:	It's a flatty-sidey thing, multiple facets but internal integrity. *(Excitedly starting to map out the different faces again with his hands.)*

A marketing colleague interrupted:

Rick:	It's a dodecahedron
Simon:	*(Hands freeze and he looks up.)* No that wouldn't be right.
Rick:	It is, it's a dodecahedron, let me sketch it for you.
Simon:	*(Drops his hands and speaks crossly.)* It isn't, and now I can't see the model I was building up.

I intervened at this point to bring the focus back on Simon and to support him to rebuild his model.

I figured that Rick had already had plenty of feedback about not staying with the other person's model, so at this stage I just wanted the session back on track.

Caitlin: **And it's got** different faces **and** scientists see one, lawyers another, **and** consistent internal structure **and** when they describe it, it has the same kind of feel ... **And is there anything else about it?**

Simon: *(Re-engages with his model using his hands and starts to talk excitedly again.)* Yes, it is a flatty sidey thing; that's the right name for it. It looks different depending on where you are standing but it's all the same thing really.

After they'd finished modelling Simon, I asked Rick about his intention in calling it a dodecahedron and he said that once it was clear in his own mind, he was more caught up with telling his vision than in helping Simon shape his.

Simon shared how this had distracted him and had ended up destroying the mental model he was building up. The flatty-sidey thing was a product that Simon was developing and the expertise about it was in him. This was a great example of when to stay completely clean and just let someone reflect on and make sense of what they already know.

> This was a great example of when to stay completely clean and just let someone reflect on and make sense of what they already know.

Advocating for competing products

Our final piece of work was about being able to articulate the benefits of one piece of software over another. The sales team wanted to be able to articulate the costs and benefits of Linux over Microsoft to their customers. They worked without my help and no one person was in charge of this process. The session was more about teasing out from one another some metaphors for why they personally preferred using Linux over Microsoft. The way that they were working together followed the same dynamic as it would if I'd been training attention on one person, then another, to build up a network of attention around the room.

One metaphor for Microsoft was like a city from the film 'Blade Runner': it looks all modern with a high tech façade but if you get too close you can see all the broken lift shafts and huge concrete graveyards of out of date architecture. The landscape is filled with leaking, unstable structures.

In contrast they described working with Linux as being like a village of pioneers, living off the land and inventing structures from scratch using materials around them. It may seem harder work but the structures are more efficient and well thought through and absolutely suit the needs of the villagers.

The team members were out of their seats and drawing throughout this process and evidently competent now to run these processes unaided. I felt like a proud parent and knew my work here was done.

What Happened Next?

The team relabelled clean questions and metaphor models as their *'common definition language'* and used the process to reflect on a whole range of areas where previously they had had difficulties. After I left, they created their own state of the art 'metaphor modelling' room filled with white boards, pens, magnets and other creative resources. This was their shared thinking space, where they elicited metaphors for products and projects in development.

When a customer had difficulty specifying their requirements, the sales team would invite them into the metaphor room where they shared examples of different metaphors for various product designs and elicit fresh ones from their clients.

It had been a joy to run the project, the BBC film crew had enjoyed it as much as we had and John Martin from the Open University had the footage and the process that he was after.

While writing this book, I reconnected with Chris and asked him what led him to take the risk of inviting me into his company and letting me loose to do clean modelling with his team. He said:

> "We weren't just about designing software; we were about working out the criteria in our software design that made us successful. Which bits were replicable and how could we put our new learning into the next design project? This was balanced with our need to make money.
>
> "Before we met you, we were modelling our external design processes but not the internal individual and group processes that allowed us to come up with these designs. That was the missing bit and that's where you came in."

This was the first time Clean Language had been taken into a business setting and I decided to call the process 'Metaphors at Work', since that described the central theme and also because I love the ambiguity in the phrase.

I wanted to test Metaphors at Work with another group who had a high degree of self-awareness and to get more feedback on the impact of going through the process. I invited the key members of our Clean Practice Group to the first Metaphors at Work training and ran it assisted by Dee, Penny and James. The process worked as successfully for people who didn't already work together as it did for a formed team. The attendees learned a lot about themselves, how they related to other people and what they'd need to do to work effectively together. We had many discussions about where else such an approach might be useful.

I might have drifted back into youth and community work after this but when the Open University ran their next MBA module in Creative Management it now included a BBC film of the Metaphors at Work process. MBA students, often quite senior managers, started contacting me and inviting me into their businesses to run the process with their teams. I shifted from being a quirky youth worker with an interest in metaphor to becoming an innovative business consultant with a clean modelling approach to culture change.

Cautionary Tale

One of the concerns I'd had while scoping this project was that once we started eliciting metaphors and helping people get in touch with their values, there might be some irreconcilable differences between people. One member of the team thoroughly enjoyed his one-to-one session but when he listened to his colleagues' metaphors for an ideal team, he became increasingly uncomfortable. He noticed a big disparity between his need for career progression and structure and their celebration of having no hierarchy and remaining small and innovative. After the first group session he resigned.

This didn't seem like a positive outcome at the time and I was nervous but Chris, true to his word, said that he'd much rather this had happened early on in this employee's time with the company. He actually saw the process as having benefits for helping people see when they don't belong in an organisation and finding work that really suits them.

From then on, I included resignations as one possible success criterion and encouraged other clients to view this as positively as Chris and Robert had.

CHAPTER 4

Working with Diversity

Supporting public sector teams and organisations to develop inclusive attitudes towards colleagues and customers

After the shift from working with disaffected kids to being accepted in the business world there was a sudden increase in demand for my Metaphors at Work process.

- Would it be useful in mergers and acquisitions?
- Can you use this with a steering group made up of volunteers?
- How would you apply this in downsizing?
- Could this work within my family?

My stock answer was "I don't know, tell me some more about the context and let's have a go and see what happens."

Despite the obvious financial and status benefits of working in the private sector, I wanted to ensure that my time was balanced between community and corporate work. There didn't seem much point trying to improve one without influencing the other.

I achieved this quite simply by going wherever I was invited, whether that was into business, a troubled family, a newly merged business team or a local community centre. Each time I ran the process, I changed little bits to see what the impact was. I didn't yet know its scope or potential; I just found the application of the process compelling, no matter who I was doing it with.

Some of the people I encountered were so taken with the process that they left their own paths and joined me on mine for a while until they had learned what they needed. My next important collaborator was Patrick Weekes, whom I'd met initially at the Youth Project. He made time to assist me on many of my projects and also invited me to contribute to some of his. This chapter is about a couple of diversity projects we ran together.

Harnessing Diversity in a Public Sector Training Team

Patrick was contacted by a centre providing training to leading public servants from two different fields. The centre was facing a number of complaints around diversity issues aimed at their mixed team of trainers. The trainers had been reprimanded and told that comments and jokes needed to stop, but it hadn't made a difference. They decided to bring in some external support to help address trainer prejudice and to create a more inclusive team. Their evidence for success would be:

- Reduction in the number of complaints.
- No racist or misogynist jokes during the training or in the breaks.
- Trainers going out of their way to make relationships with minority delegates.
- More minority delegates applying for the training.

I was very excited to be invited along because of the complexity of the issue. The trainers came from very different organisational cultures and one of the ways that they bonded was by making jokes about people who weren't like them.

Both the trainers and trainees also had to make critical decisions when out in the field, sometimes based on very little information – and making the right decision was often a matter of life and death. I wondered how open they'd be to developing the state of curiosity and not-knowing that goes with taking on a clean approach.

Starting from Curiosity Rather than Contempt

While the goal of most diversity programmes is honourable – that people are respected at work and that customers are offered an equal level of service – they often start from the legal position that you're not allowed to be racist, sexist, ageist etc. If you are, then you are holding colleagues and customers in contempt and therefore you are in contempt of the law.

But everyone stereotypes, has prejudice and discriminates. It's part of what it means to be social animals. Not holding any prejudice and never discriminating means being in a constant state of not knowing.

Demanding that an organisation be free from prejudice and discrimination means you're already setting people up to deny, lie about, and hide behaviours and feelings that they're going to be doing anyway. This is more likely to prevent them from seeking out and forming relationships with people who are unlike them, in case they inadvertently get things wrong. The law isn't necessarily the best place to start.

I already had lots of evidence that people were able to change dramatically when we started group sessions from a position of curiosity and respect and I wanted to bring that approach into this intervention.

Leading by Example

Patrick and I decided to get curious about our own prejudice and discrimination first, much as Dee and I had done with our modelling skills in the early days. We shared prejudices we had about one another, things that irritated us and the things we made up about one another's backgrounds.

Out of this self-reflection came a whole raft of learning and it was amazing how much of our time we had been spending in complete fantasy about what the other person was thinking or doing. We turned all of this learning into stories that we later used during the diversity training.

As well as being interested in our own stereotyping and prejudice, we also wanted to explore what makes some people stop discriminating and to form real connections with people who are unlike them. Again we started with our own patterns.

Caitlin: **What makes you seek out diversity?**

Patrick: I'm just curious about people.

Caitlin: **What kind of** curious?

Patrick: I'm intrigued. I want to know how they tick, what's important to them.

Caitlin: **Whereabouts is** intrigued?

Patrick: Like a pull between us.

Caitlin: **And** a pull between us, **and** you're curious, **then what happens?**

Patrick: I go and talk to them.

Caitlin: **What happens just before** you go and talk to them – **what is it that allows you to do that?**

Patrick: I feel confident. I've always been good with people. I see it as a challenge to find something we've got in common.

Caitlin: **Then what happens?**

Patrick: I observe them, work out what's important to them and then find something I can genuinely connect with. That enriches me.

Patrick: **What about you?**

Caitlin: I don't necessarily feel confident, but I feel duty-bound.

Patrick: **What kind of** duty-bound?

Caitlin: I feel that as a human being, if I sense in myself fear or ignorance regarding another person, I need to go and do something about it.

Patrick: **Where does** duty-bound **come from?**

Caitlin: My grandma was a Unitarian Universalist and took me to her church in Florida when I was a teenager. She introduced me to Atheists, Christians, African Americans, Jews, a group of Biker Dykes visiting from New York and she challenged me to sense any discomfort I had and to keep expanding my social group until it included the whole human race.

Patrick: **And when you sense there's** discomfort **or** ignorance, **then what happens?**

Caitlin: I know if I don't make the effort, there will always be a schism in my mind between me and them and I'll feel ashamed, like I've let Grandma down. I feel I must address it and find something that means I can reach across and make a connection with that other person.

As we modelled one another, we observed that neither of us was afraid to admit that we had prejudices. We did try to address them but we didn't feel ashamed of having them. We decided that acknowledging prejudice would be crucial to this project and knew we'd have to present the idea iteratively, starting with our own prejudice, then prejudice in general before encouraging them to join in.

We incorporated all of this into a simple two-day diversity modelling process:

Day 1

A: Invite people to model what it means to stereotype, have prejudice and discriminate.

B: Use our own stories (about prejudices we used to have about each other) to get the group comfortable with admitting that they've been prejudiced in the past.

Day 2

C: Invite people to model how they've naturally updated a prejudice and what motivated them to do that.

D: Have them share prejudices they still hold.

E: Take the learning from C and apply it to the prejudices in D.

F: What actions can you take now?

Clean questions, when used in any context, begin to elicit metaphors such as Patrick's *pull between us* and my *schism in my mind*. These conversational metaphors allow us to self-model and help us to make models of one another's experience. However, this was the first project where we wouldn't be explicitly asking our clients to develop overt metaphors and I wondered whether this would impact on its success.

Day 1

We arrived on the first day and there were 12 senior trainers in the group. The morning session was all about exploring the topic non-judgementally and Patrick and I shared one of my prejudices. As we went along we invited the group to join in the tale.

Caitlin: Do you know, when I'm walking along, talking to Patrick, he never gives me eye contact.

And we stood up and demonstrated, walking across the room with me talking to Patrick and him looking away from me.

Caitlin: And no matter how important the discussion is to me, he never really pays attention. I know he's not listening to me because he looks away.

Patrick: *(To the group)* How many people here would know that that meant I really wasn't listening to her?

One guy said that he wouldn't trust someone who didn't give eye contact.

Caitlin: Who thinks he is listening to me?

Another guy from Ireland said that not having eye contact doesn't mean you aren't listening.

We were holding, live in the room, the simple idea that one behaviour can have at least two different inferences. We were legitimising this idea from the start.

Caitlin: OK, here's what happened next.

I continued walking around the room with him and got more irritated saying,

Caitlin: Look Patrick, if you don't want me to tell you about this idea now, we can do it some other time.

Patrick: No, this is a great time. Carry on.

As I leaned round trying to catch his eye, demonstrating how frustrated I used to get, he started turning away from me and said to the group "This really happened once in Oxford Street!"

Patrick: So I'm thinking, she's getting irritated with me and I don't really know what's happening but now we seem to be turning around and going the other way. We must have been going the wrong way. Now we're walking back down Oxford Street. She's getting more irritated. I'm confused, and I'm irritated now, and I don't even know where we're going.

We stopped and asked the group to comment on what was happening and they had a discussion about eye contact and whose wife kept turning round to talk to him in the car instead of looking at the road and whose dad used to belt him for looking him in the eye.

This was all quite easy stuff and the group was quite comfortable so we took it up a level. Patrick is black and I'm white so I brought in a past prejudice to illustrate our point.

Caitlin: I've read in a diversity training manual that black boys often find it hard to give eye contact and you shouldn't expect them to.

And there was a bit of a, "Hurr?" in the group.

Caitlin: When he turns away, I just think, "Do you know what? It's in his culture; he just doesn't give eye contact. Black men don't give eye contact. So I shouldn't expect him to. It's a different culture to mine." Well, I dropped by his house one Saturday and I was invited in. His family were having a barbecue. His mum was serving me food and I noticed a whole line of men sat against a wall. They were all looking forward while they were talking. I thought, "Oh look, that's where he gets it from. His family aren't listening to each other either. They're all talking but no-one's really listening." I felt compassionate about Patrick and understood it wasn't his fault.

But then one man was telling a story and the whole of this line started laughing. And I noticed what fantastic rapport they all had with one another. They were obviously having a good time together and communicating effortlessly. But that couldn't be possible because they weren't paying respectful attention to each other.

And then something ugly happened in my system where I had to think, "Hang on a minute. I've got this all wrong. I've been asking the wrong questions. When I look at Patrick while I'm talking and he looks away, I ask, "Why aren't you listening to me?" It's always from a position of what I'm doing is OK but what he's doing isn't OK."

And so, the next time we were at work, I said "Patrick, when I'm speaking to you, and you look down and to your left, what's happening?"

Patrick and I retook up our positions walking across the room.

Patrick: Oh, I'm giving you ear contact.
Caitlin: **What kind of** ear-contact?
Patrick: I'm making sense of what you're saying, taking it in through my ear and building a sort of a 3D model of what you're talking about, in space.
Caitlin: **Whereabouts is that** 3D model?
Patrick: Kind of down to my left.
Caitlin: **OK so, when you're doing that and I walk around and stand in front of you like this, what happens?"**

He turned away from me.

Patrick: Well you get in the way and the model gets destroyed and I have to turn away to create some more space to think in and start again.

At this stage we invited the group to get into threes and chat about the story and what it meant. We didn't really mind too much what they thought at this stage; we were more interested in demonstrating that it was OK to share and explore a prejudice and for the other person not to get offended.

Next we used the Five Senses exercise to set the tone for legitimising difference and demonstrating that people can be surprised by their own thoughts.

From here we went straight into exploring the terms *stereotype, prejudice* and *discrimination*. We put one of these terms in the middle of the room, asked the group what it meant, someone answered, we asked a couple of clean questions and moved on to someone else. We kept moving around the group until there was a shared sense of what they all thought. To ensure they didn't start answering the same way we asked questions like, "So who thinks something different?" and "Who isn't like that?" At this stage we were more interested in differences than similarities.

Once the group had explored the terms and understood the subject, we asked them to share their personal experiences of being stereotyped or of other people being prejudiced about them.

Patrick: **What's a stereotype someone might have about you?**
Adrian: Southerner!
Patrick: **What kind of** Southerner?
Adrian: Posh.

Patrick: **Who's different to that?**
Sandy: They call me a Jock!
Patrick: **Is there anything else about** Jock?
Sandy: Scottish, ginger and tight.

Caitlin: **What's a prejudice someone might have about you?**
Mark: I'm really big and people think I'm going to be dangerous.
Caitlin: **What kind of** dangerous?
Mark: **They're scared of me, they tell me later when they know me better.**

Caitlin: **Who's not like that?**
Adrian: When I first joined, I know people thought that I thought I was better than them; they used to make sly comments.
Caitlin: **Then what happened?**
Adrian: I called them on it, made them stop.

The content for the training was now coming from the group rather than from us and Patrick and I kept each other in check and made sure we didn't answer for them. We just asked one or two clean questions of any answer we received. This way, we got them used to bouncing ideas and answers around the group and all of their answers were accepted and included.

That first day was exploratory, light and relatively easy. At first the group were reticent to talk but by the afternoon session they started to comment on one another's answers without being asked to.

We left them at the end of that day with the question, "What's a prejudice you used to have but lost?" Patrick and I were both unsure of how well the processes had worked and whether they would lead to any lasting change in behaviour.

Day 2

The next morning they came back in, took their seats and we started with "So what's a prejudice you used to have but lost?" One of the participants who'd been very quiet so far, started immediately:

Brian: I used to hate the Germans. I spent my childhood listening to my Grandad talk about the Luftwaffe and his experiences in the air force and I saw all Germans as enemies. If I heard about them in the news or met them I was filled with feelings of hate. Then when Grandad died and I went through all his war memorabilia, I realised that he didn't hate them; he hated what they were doing. He was actually in admiration of their planes, their battle techniques and their soldiers.
Caitlin: **What difference did this make?**
Brian: I could hold hate and admiration in the same place and I started to get interested in Germans and German history. I've since visited Germany and got German friends. It's become a hobby of mine too, a link to my Granddad.

This turned out to be a floodgate for personal stories.

Mark: Do you know what? I used to hate Asians, hate them. I used to think, "They're fucking everywhere. They've taken over Liverpool; they've just stolen our way of life." I would bitch about it in pubs and stir it up with my mates.

Caitlin: **Then what happened?**

Mark: I was posted, with the army, to East Africa and my kid made friends with an Asian kid at the school whose dad was posted out there. I got to know their family, we became friends, had them over for dinner and we're still good friends now. I started to loosen it and now when I meet Asians, I'm more likely to assume they're friendly – and they usually are.

Patrick: **What motivated you to update your prejudice?**

Mark: Just the contact, no more than that – I had to have some reason for getting to know them and then I could see them as real people.

Patrick: **Where did the prejudice come from?**

Mark: Actually I've been thinking about this since yesterday. What happened was I went into the army when I was seventeen. I left Liverpool and I was away for most of five years and when I came back, there'd been an Asian influx in Liverpool and they'd taken over some market stalls in the area where I lived. I felt they'd changed my hometown, but actually it was nothing to do with them. In the time I'd been away I'd changed so much I couldn't relate to the people I'd left behind. I'd grown out of my own neighbourhood. Asians became symbolic of the fact that I didn't feel at home when I came home.

One story led to another. One guy sat up and joined in:

Sandy: Oh right, OK, well let me tell you, I used to hate disabled people. Hate them. I used to think if they can't walk then why are they fucking driving? I used to park in disabled parking bays because I'd just think "sod them".

Patrick: **Then what happened?**

Sandy: Well quite late in life I met the woman that I love. I was in my forties when I met her and she's wonderful. For the first time I really know what it's like to connect with somebody.

And these were big blokes' blokes but no one laughed at one another. Just like with the youth project, when people tell these personal stories, it's a sacred space and the group just listen respectfully to one another.

Sandy: Shortly after our marriage, she developed MS and has been declining ever since. I understand completely now why there are disabled parking bays. Every day, every extra step that she has to take is absolute agony for her. Listening to Mark talk about Asians, I've been thinking about where my hatred of disabled drivers came from. The only disabled person I'd seen growing up was Joey Deacon, from Blue Peter, who my parents used to make fun of. If I did or said something wrong they'd slap their wrists and be all, "Eurgh, eurgh, eurgh, Joey!" at me. As kids, we used to really take the piss out of people by pretending they were spastic. It was all twisted arms and grunting and laughing at each other. I was terrified I'd get to an accident scene with a disabled person in it, and I would be so embarrassed I wouldn't know how to deal with them. I wouldn't want to touch them. I was so horrified I had this idea that I didn't want them in cars.'

The group began to unpack not just how they had lost some of their prejudices but also the psychological and sociological processes that caused them to form in the first place. The realisations they were having were very similar to the kinds of insights people have when they are uncovering their personal metaphors and listening to other people's. I realised that the success must be due to the quality of attention in the group.

It was pure poetry to watch; remembering it still makes me smile. It's also indicative of how much awareness and intelligence was available to this group, it was just untapped.

They spent the afternoon of that second day looking at the factors that led to them updating their prejudice and how they could incorporate those factors into their training programmes. They talked about increasing personal contact between participants rather than it all coming from the trainers, getting people to share their history and how they'd come to train at their centre. They planned to run the stereotyping, prejudice and discrimination exercise and ask people to think about when their prejudice got in the way of making good decisions in the field.

There'd been no telling the group what to do or what to think, just non-judgemental modelling of what had happened, what was happening and what they wanted to have happen next. This process seemed to inspire capability in the group and encourage them to move to action.

A thought that comes to mind on re-reading this case study is that it was about meeting people where they were, not where we might wish they were. Between the non-judgemental attention, the clean questions and the design of the day there was space for change to happen almost effortlessly.

> It was about meeting people where they were, not where we might wish they were.

The question for us then was how to begin to talk about the changing we were noticing. When Patrick was invited to tender for a piece of work in a UK National Health Service Trust, a much bigger piece of work with 900 members of staff, this offered us the opportunity to train a few more diversity facilitators and to evaluate the impact of the process across a much wider group.

A National Health Service Trust of around 900 people

Discrimination laws meant that it wasn't just undesirable to have a staff that discriminated against colleagues and patients, it was against the law and complaints that were upheld could cost the Trust a lot of money. The Trust wanted staff who understood the law and complied with it. We didn't want to start with the law, for reasons already given, so we proposed an intervention that still had modelling at its core and brought the law and the need for compliance into the second session.

The process we ran was the same as for the training centre except that there would be just two half-days, separated by a week. This meant we had to cut some of the exercises short. The personal development wouldn't be quite as deep but we hoped the shift in thinking across the staff team would still be significant.

The project sponsors were the Diversity Awareness Board, who proposed that everyone in the organisation should do the training and that every training group should be a mix of board members, health-care assistants, doctors, porters, nurses etc. – a kind of diagonal slice through the organisation. This seemed a great idea because it meant the discussion would always include a mix of perceptions from across the trust.

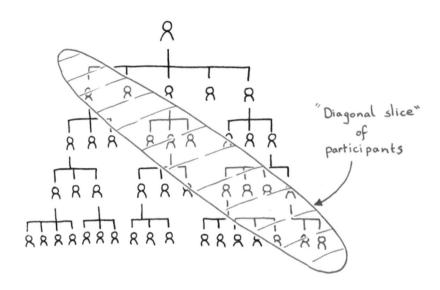

"Diagonal slice" of participants

We invited Nancy Doyle, an occupational psychologist, to help us evaluate the impact of our approach. We wanted to investigate what would happen to the attention of people as they went through the process. Prior to the training, she interviewed a cross-section of participants to find out what diversity awareness meant for them. What did they expect to happen in the training? What were they hoping it was going to be like? She planned to interview them before the course began, after the first session and again a while after the second session.

Because this was quite a large project, we invited some trainees into our team and this meant another round of self-modelling, revealing a whole range of new prejudices. We tried to make our training team as diverse as possible to reflect the diversity of our clients and we especially selected people who were different from both Patrick and I.

While we were considering typical diversity issues such as gender, sexual orientation or race, we were also sorting for people with very different patterns around memory, conflict resolution, organisation, etc. These can cause just as much prejudice and discrimination at work as anything else. These differences are also great places to start the training from.

Once again we started these sessions with ourselves and our own issues.

Patrick: **Who here knows that the best way to resolve a work based conflict is to give it some space and let things cool down and talk about it the next day?**

Some people put their hands up, laughed and agreed.

Caitlin: **Who here knows it's best to sort it out there and then to stop it festering?**

A different group of people laughed and nodded. By sharing and exploring these little differences it was easy to move on to the bigger issues.

During the second session, after sharing which factors led to them updating their prejudice, participants were asked what they'd noticed between sessions. Staff confessed to leaving certain people out of their team activities, shared stories of patients who discriminated against them and revealed gaps in their knowledge of other cultures. They started to talk more openly of larger scale discrimination issues they'd noticed between different areas of personnel, such as nurses against doctors, ward managers against senior managers.

We acknowledged every contribution, asking one or two clean questions to expand their thinking. We would ask the group to comment on what they were hearing and invited them to bring in a different experience or share their expertise. We wanted the group to become their own experts and to make more use of their own diversity.

A: Is it true that Muslim men don't like female nurses touching them?

B: Yes in my family they wouldn't want to touch a woman they weren't related to.

Caitlin: **Who's not like that?**

D: That's not true for us; I think it must depend on how you interpret religion.

A: Well how will I know?

B: You could ask the patient?

Once they were approaching the problem as a group, we brought in the issue of discrimination laws saying, "Given that you are prejudiced, and you have been discriminating and been discriminated against, and you all have to comply with the law, what would you like to have happen now?"

The group started to design small discrete Developmental Tasks that were completely within their control and that they were willing to do. Some would be half-formed ideas and their colleagues would build on them. Some would be problems and their colleagues would give examples of what had worked in other areas. We knew we'd done a good job when the group stopped looking to our team for guidance and got into action-orientated conversations with one another.

This is another example of the implicit use of the Karma Cycle. Our new team of facilitators were helping groups to unpack what they wanted to have happen, what was actually happening, what they were making up about it and what they could do next to build better relationships at work.

Evaluation

Nancy evaluated this diversity awareness course using questionnaires and Clean Interviewing techniques to make sure that she minimised her influence over the participants' answers. She did a content analysis of their answers, to explore themes that emerged across a majority of the answers.

The responses people gave *before* the training read very much like an equal opportunities policy. They referred to groups of people who are often discriminated against, such as ethnic minorities and women. Their answers contained no action – no one was talking about what they could do differently. Nancy summarised this as a 'third person' understanding of diversity: how it refers to 'other' people.

The responses gathered *during* the training were markedly different. People were no longer referring to large groups of 'other' people, but instead talking about each other. They were referring to the diversity that existed between themselves, their colleagues and the other people on the course. Nancy summarised this a second person position: how am I different to you?

After the training was completed, the group shifted in perspective again. Now, the feedback was characterised by action: What can I do to make a difference, to celebrate diversity, to bridge gaps? Nancy summarised this as a first person understanding of diversity. A couple of examples of this are:

Nurse: It really annoys me that I've got three Nigerian colleagues who all start speaking their language together, and I feel really left out and upset. I've let it build up over the years. I skimp on the handover with them and I noticed last week that I look for things they do wrong so I can bitch about them to my friend. This week, I'm going to ask them to speak English when we first get together so I can join in and we can have a cup of tea together while we do the handover and then they can speak their language afterwards. This way I know I can do a better job for our patients.

Manager: I've noticed I make everyone a cup of tea except Jan. I can't even remember how it started but I always leave her out. I don't know anything about her - not even how many kids she has. So yesterday, I went and asked her if I could make her a cup of tea, and she said she doesn't drink tea. I said, can I make you something else and she said she would love a glass of cold water. So now she's included in the tea ritual. None of us knew she felt left out; we just thought she liked to keep herself to herself. I'm going to look around and find other places that I'm leaving people out and ask them whether they're happy or what they'd like instead.

The shift away from diversity as something to do with other people and towards an attitude of "What can I do about this right now?" is a regular, enduring result of this approach and one we have seen replicated in all of the case studies.

In the health service diversity project I'd been impressed that the leaders of the organisations were in the same training groups as the staff and that the whole organisation was trying to change at the same time. It avoided the issues I'd had at the youth project where change and development were limited to a small area and not supported by the wider system.

After this I became more and more focussed on whether the leaders commissioning change projects and the facilitators delivering those projects were willing to undergo and be examples of the change work themselves. It felt intuitively wrong to be asking groups of people to do as I say but not as I do.

Cautionary Tale

Approaching any problem from a modelling rather than a training perspective requires a deep commitment to personal development because, wherever you need your clients to go, you have to be prepared to go there yourself. It isn't enough to tell people what

> Wherever you need your clients to go, you have to be prepared to go there yourself.

they should do, you need to be able to demonstrate not only that you do it yourself, but also to be able to articulate how it has benefited you in a way that makes sense to your client.

If I really wanted my groups to be open to exploring and giving up some of their deep-seated prejudices then I would have to address my own no matter how attached I was to them – especially the ones I believed were fundamentally true.

I was very lucky to have great mentors in David, Penny, James, Dee and Chris who helped me to address the patterns I couldn't uncover on my own. I was also very lucky to have great playmates, like Patrick, who were also on this journey of personal and professional development. We held the value of applying the processes to ourselves before we took them to our clients. This didn't mean that we were always successful and we often had to learn on the job, but we were open to feedback, learning and change.

The benefit was that with each fear and irritation we were able to notice, share and unpack, we learned so much about who we were and where each of us was coming from and then found a compromise from which we could grow in our understanding of ourselves and one another.

CHAPTER 5

Code Congruence

Designing a whole 'Welfare to Work' company based on clean principles

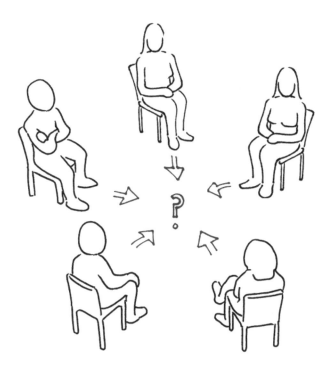

So, I could use this methodology I was developing with individuals, groups, small companies and large workforces. All the groups we worked with seemed to move away from contempt, towards curiosity and into action. Now that I had some guidelines, some principles and a few models that contributed to these changes, what would I like to have happen next?

How about helping a client set up a company from scratch, using Systemic Modelling™ as a core methodology?

In this chapter I'll discuss the process I developed, assisted by Patrick, for working with the long term unemployed and how the opportunity to move from delivering the process to supporting the set up of a new Welfare to Work (W2W) company came about. Although the story is specific to one industry, the processes that came out of it can and have been used in a wide range of private and public sectors.

A senior manager in the W2W industry commissioned me to develop a unique course that could engage the hardest to help, long-term unemployed adults with multiple barriers to finding work in East London. I designed an approach that was very similar to the one I'd used at the youth project but now I utilised the other models and learning that I'd developed along the way.

Working with the unemployed created an interesting bind. On the one hand I was commissioned to help these people to change their behaviour and attitudes and on the other hand I was using an approach that said on no account could I dictate to people how they should change or even that they should change. I explained to Richard that I wouldn't take an expert position in the group or try to motivate them. I would be accepting them just as they were, without any contempt. I would role-model paying exquisite attention, self-discovery and curiosity but any actual change would have to come from the group themselves. Richard was curious and interested and had the foresight to take a risk and said he'd take care of the job outcome rates if I could get the groups engaged.

I invited Patrick to join me and first we shared our own outcomes, hopes and dreams for the course and modelled our own job-seeking and life changing skills and strategies. Then we started with 18 adults who'd been told they would have their benefits stopped if they didn't attend these 'motivational' courses. We gave the group a brief overview of the course, then went straight into a Clean Set Up to get their outcomes and attitudes into the open. These could vary drastically:

Caitlin: **If this course were to be really useful for you, it will be like what?**

- Nothing, I don't want to be here.
- Fun and friendly and I'd like some job search techniques.
- I just want to socialise, meet some new people.
- I want to work in retail, I want to find out how to get in to this work.
- There aren't any jobs anyway so you're just wasting my time.
- I need interview practice.
- I want to find out what work I want. I'm lost.

We accepted everyone's position and just went into the Five Senses exercise, then 'Time' and 'Working at our best' and continued modelling whatever came up in the group.

Instead of managing the group's behaviour and learning, Patrick and I were very strict with one another about the rules for getting the system to self-model. If one of us started to try persuading someone to join in or turn someone's negative answer into a positive outcome, then the other one would bring this directly to the group's attention.

Patrick: **Shall I tell you what I'm noticing? Caitlin's asked Ashad what he'd like to have happen and he's said he is going to sit in the corner with his headphones on. Now Caitlin's saying that that means he won't benefit from the course. And I'm wondering if she really meant to ask Ashad what he wanted or whether she's trying to persuade him to do something. What do you think?**

Nikki: Oh well we're all joining in so it's rude for him to take himself off in the corner.

Patrick: **Who's different again?**

Caleb: Allow him, if that's what he wants to do.

This way we'd keep demonstrating that there wasn't a top-down rule for what was right and wrong but as a group they could hear how their behaviour was viewed by other people and make their own decisions about what they would do next.

We needed to train ourselves and them from feeling that someone else should take responsibility for their behaviour. We also fed back patterns that we noticed to the group about their behaviour. For example:

Caitlin: **We're noticing that 15 of you arrive at nine thirty and three of you come in at ten thirty. Can I check, what would you all like to have happen about when we start?**

One group member said that it made no difference to him, he didn't mind what other people did. Then we'd ask, "Who's not feeling like that?" Another said that it wasn't fair that people were late as then they had to explain the exercises twice and it was wasting everyone else's time. And we'd keep moving around the group. Someone else said that they were forced to come on the course or they'd lose their benefits, but no one could force them to be there all day.

We opened it up to the group to negotiate a compromise, "So when *you're* frustrated at having things explained twice and *you* don't want to be here all day, what could happen now?" The later ones agreed to come by ten and the early ones would do some open questions or work on their CVs from nine thirty until ten. We were always looking for a group response to the situation rather than imposing control ourselves.

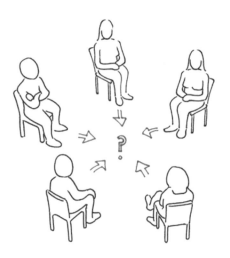

By the afternoon of the first day around half of the group were engaging in the debates and then in the exercises and making their own rules or compromises about phone use or punctuality. By the second afternoon we had most of the group involved. Even the one or two who absolutely refused to join in on the first day usually turned up on the second and third until one specific exercise caught their attention and they joined in.

We always followed the principle of group members meeting one another where they were rather than where they wished they were. One young woman set herself a Developmental Task simply to speak audibly in front of the group once in a session. There wasn't much else that could happen work-wise until she'd managed that and the group were all right behind her. She started in small groups and then in the breaks and then when she did speak in the group there'd be a supportive cheer that made her laugh until it was the norm. A young man with two first class degrees in engineering and physics who had been unemployed for five years, was given the feedback that whenever he talked to people he stared at the ceiling and then wandered off topic so that they were bored. He was set, by the group, the task to make eye contact and to check every few moments whether they understood him. In turn, they'd smile and nod to encourage him.

The most important aspect of these courses was that the group were making great use of their own skills and expertise from the very start and this bred confidence and inspired capability that they could change their circumstances.

My check for whether we were running the course well was whether Patrick and I would both find value from being sent on it ourselves. Would it be as beneficial for a teacher or a bank manager as it was for this target group? If so, then we were probably along the right lines.

The courses received great feedback and I was still loving what I was doing. Richard liked our style and his advisors said that when the clients returned from these courses they were much more enthusiastic and 'job-focussed'. But, despite the enthusiasm, I kept saying to Richard, "The thing is, we're creating a programme here which inspires people to feel more able to articulate their needs and more capable of achieving them, but then they're going back to employment advisors who don't have the skills or attitude to follow it up. They try to force clients into any old job just to hit their targets. Within a couple of weeks clients are heading back to square one. That's not sustainable."

Richard took my point and looked for opportunities for us to deliver Metaphors at Work and 'Diversity at Work' across the UK for some of his staff teams. I still felt as though we were being parachuted in to solve a problem but never able to impact on the system as a whole. Then a fantastic opportunity presented itself.

A Whole New Organisation

Richard was invited to develop a new Welfare to Work organisation with an Australian company who were bidding for contracts in the UK. If they won the contract, he could recruit, induct and train the team just the way he wanted to. He called and said, "If we were going to create an organisation from scratch that put these principles into practice, how would we go about it?"

How brilliant was this? I sat with him at a venue in central London and after asking some modelling questions about how the whole thing would work and the attitudes and values he wanted at the core, I began modelling and once I had enough information I proceeded to describe his model and my model with my hands and to draw it all out on scraps of paper.

He needed a high performing team who could hit the ground running and achieve high targets in a short space of time. I needed the team to be as diverse as the clients they were supporting so that they could use one another to update their prejudice and practise reducing discrimination. This way they could build great relationships with everyone who came through their door.

We would recruit people who were open to feedback, learning and personal development since they'd be asking clients to be open to the same. Richard had some fantastic ideas for physicalising this way of working; staff would be in learning teams of six and every six weeks would reform into different groupings so that their learning never went stale and they could practise sharing their caseloads.

I suggested a staff induction process that had the same structure as the client training course. This way it would be 'the way we do things around here' from the moment people joined the company. They wouldn't be asking their clients to do anything they hadn't done themselves. The induction process would serve as team building for the diverse staff AND

> It would be 'the way we do things around here' from the moment people joined the company.

would help them in developing the skills to build rapport with diverse clients.

Occasionally, Richard and I got into wrangles and debates. He would argue that getting people into work was still the core of the company and what they were paid for so this had to be at the heart of the client training course. I argued that even having that as an unspoken outcome during the training would shift the group focus from self-managing to being managed.

Richard wanted to allot separate coffee areas for staff and clients; I argued that this would create a physical divide between clients and staff and a 'them and us' feel and was incongruent with his value of treating clients as equals.

Wisely, I'd engaged Penny and James to help the two of us get a shared model. With their help we clarified each other's positions and found compromises we were both happy with. For example, I agreed to design more job-focussed activities and he agreed that staff and clients would use the same coffee machine.

Ten years later he says that the phrase he most associates with this project is, "Richard, can I just check? Is that process *congruent* with what you want to have happen?"

Codifying the Process

It was at this stage that I realised I needed help in codifying the processes I was running. It wasn't going to be enough for me to keep all of the information in my head and for Patrick and I to know instinctively how to facilitate the group. It needed to be written down in a manual so that it could be replicated by the company after we left. I invited Nancy Doyle to jump off her corporate career ladder in recruitment and to join us more fully in this project. I wanted someone on board with an occupational psychology approach who could describe and evaluate what we were doing as the project developed. She observed both the design and the approach, wrote down the exercises and began to help codify the whole approach. Her creativity and competence were a big factor in the successes of the next few years.

Modelling Excellence in W2W

Richard chose three advisors he felt were the epitome of excellence in getting people into work and treating clients with respect while hitting high targets. I set about modelling them, asking about their behaviours, beliefs and metaphors to uncover their unconscious approaches. After we analysed the data for patterns and themes we had a description of the attitudes and aptitudes we wanted in the new workforce. Now we could start recruiting this amazing group of staff.

We designed a unique, new Clean Recruitment process including job descriptions, preparation questions, an interview, an aptitude test, and a half day in an assessment centre. Our company, Training Attention, would run the assessment centre and the three exemplary advisors, along with Richard, would run the interviews. The assessment centres were an opportunity for small groups of applicants to come together, go through a series of exercises and demonstrate their attitudes and rapport building skills in person.

Clean Recruitment

Before candidates came to their interview, we asked them the following questions:

- When you're working at your best, you're like what?
- An ideal team for you, that would support you to work at your best, would be like what?
- If this company were to be just as you'd like, it will be like what?

Once they arrived, we invited them to get into pairs, share their metaphors and ask a few questions about one another's models. We asked them to find out what their partner's metaphor might mean for the way they might behave at work.

During this process we observed their social interactions and looked for *congruence* and *incongruence* between what candidates said they were like and the way they actually acted with each other. We weren't demanding that they always be congruent but when we observed incongruence and brought it to their attention we were actively selecting for people who were open to feedback and to learning about themselves rather than being defensive or manipulative.

> We looked for congruence and incongruence between what candidates said they were like and the way they actually acted with each other.

Recruitment was an odd shift for me because so far I'd been modelling for the group's learning and development. Now I was modelling to make predictions about people and then offer them a job, or not, based on what I was predicting. For this reason alone we were more rigorous than ever.

This was the first example of Clean Recruitment so I'll share a couple of patterns I observed and predictions I made that meant someone didn't get selected for a second interview.

Two candidates were interviewing one another to find out their metaphors for working at their best and to demonstrate their interview and rapport building skills.

A: When I'm working at my best I'm the early bird that catches the worm.

B: I don't know what this metaphor means or how it's relevant to the job.

Caitlin: *(to B)* **Ask her some of these clarifying questions** *(indicating some cleanish questions on the wall)* **to find out a bit more about the** early bird **and then see if it becomes clearer.**

B: So what kind of early bird are you?

A: I was early for this assessment day, I filled in my preparation sheet a week early, I always get things done ahead of time so that I'm the first in line and I can see all the opportunities that others miss. That's my kind of motto.

B: *(to me)* Yeah but she's just saying that because she wants to make a good impression with you.

Although it was only twice, I was now alert to how this candidate had moved to contempt about the other person.

Caitlin: **She may be doing that, she may not. Your task at the moment is to find out more about what she is saying. We can explore whether it's true or not later on.**

B: Yeah well I don't trust her so I don't see the point of asking her any more questions.

If she were to become an advisor, she would have people in front of her who might be adept at lying or they might say things that don't make sense to her. If, when she's not sure whether something's true, she disengages then she's hardly likely to be able to engage this client group.

A different candidate was a guy who'd come with a glowing reference from his interview, they thought he'd be an ideal advisor. While we were observing him during the Five Senses exercise, we noticed that he jumped in and answered for other people rather than noticing answers and asking questions. It was a little thing at this stage but enough to warrant us deciding to give him more attention in the next exercise.

His metaphor for working at his best was that he was an open door, always ready to listen to others and to help them if he could. He was fine as the interviewee and then it was his turn to ask the questions:

B: So when you're working at your best, you're like what?

A: I'm like a well-organised shed.

B: Yeah, being organised is really important to me as well. My desk is spotless.

Then the interview stalled and they sat in silence. I stepped in and asked where they were up to.

B: Oh I know what he's like, he's just like me. We're done.

Caitlin: **There are still eight minutes of the exercise left. Use the time to find out as much as you can about this other person. Ask any of these kinds of questions here** *(indicating cleanish questions on the wall)*.

B: So you're a shed and you're really organised, does that help you to achieve more in your day?

A: Yeah, I don't like to finish my day until everything's kind of put back where it goes.

B: Yeah I hate people who just nip off at 5pm and leave a load of stuff for tomorrow. Sometimes I'm in the office till 7pm. I think I'm just really dedicated. It's the way I was raised, to finish what I've started or it niggles at me.

There was long pause and then I wandered back over from where I'd been listening.

Caitlin: **I'm noticing that you asked him one question and now you're talking about how you organise things.**

B: Yes but I get what he's like, we'd just be going round in circles.

This was the third opportunity he'd had to indicate interest in learning about others so I put a minus in that box and wrote down my evidence. If someone else were to gather evidence that he was interested in others, we'd open it up for debate later.

The crux of Clean Recruitment is to keep your observations based on what you've seen and heard and to be very clear about how you've arrived at your inferences.

My Own Unconscious Prejudice

The evidence-based assessment sheets proved to be highly illuminating. A co-facilitator, Lynne Cooper, and I discussed who from our group we thought should be invited to second interview and who was out of the running. One young man was her top candidate but a low reserve on my list. To be honest, I couldn't really remember him. She said, "But he was great, he had that brilliant insight into how 'someone who was a marksman firing straight at their target might find it difficult to work with people who didn't set goals'. Come on, he had blonde hair, very light blue eyes, tall and chatty."

Once I read her evidence, I could vaguely remember that yes, he had done all the right things and been open and curious and interested and interesting – but I hadn't noticed him. We went through some other of my marking sheets and an uncomfortable pattern emerged; if people were blonde or strawberry blonde with blue eyes, particularly if they had pale eyebrows and lashes, I was more likely to record that I had no evidence that they were either good or poor candidates. I was simply tuning them out. This was a complete surprise to me and not something I'd noticed before.

I started to wonder where it was coming from and also what I could do about it. I thought about being born in Nigeria, where the majority of the time I was with adults and children with dark skin pigmentation. Even my parents, who have pale skin, both have black hair and dark brown eyes. I'm more used to darker features. I wonder if I find it difficult to read the expressions of blonde people and therefore their contributions aren't recorded as easily in my memory.

Either way, this unconscious prejudice was costing these people their jobs. I immediately set myself a Developmental Task to pay more attention to the paler members of the group. I also shared this pattern with the other recruiters so that they could keep me at my learning edge.

Clean Induction

From this rigorous process, we had our forty-strong staff team and I took everything I knew so far about getting a group to self-model and put it into a ten-day induction course. Now both the clients and the advisors would have the same set of skills to build strong respectful relationships across the organisation with an aim of supporting people into sustainable employment that really suited them.

Just as Richard wanted clients to become less dependent on external agencies for support, it was also important to Training Attention that the W2W company would become independent of us.

Training Internal Trainers

I asked Richard to create six positions in the company for internal trainers who could deliver the Clean Induction and clean training for staff and clients. We already had an intuition that we needed at least six people in a group to get the diversity we needed for them to become a self-modelling group.

The six trainees first went through their Clean Induction with the rest of the staff team to develop awareness of themselves, their peers and how to work together.

Secondly, I invited them to attend the ten-day client training course, with the first wave of public clients, again simply as participants. This meant they could see how these exercises were received by the long-term unemployed and to see first-hand how quickly the group dynamic changed from hostile to engaged. This also had the meta-message that they and their clients were all on similar journeys of development and reduced the possibility that they would think of their clients as inferior to them.

On the third iteration these trainers delivered the course in collaboration with either Patrick or I and on the fourth they delivered independently in threes giving one another feedback and setting themselves and one another Developmental Tasks as the course progressed.

This four-iteration learning cycle seemed an ideal way to pick up and practise clean modelling with groups. Every iteration involved a high level of observation and feedback and required the trainees to set Developmental Tasks to improve their flexibility.

The trainers often felt torn between the rules of modelling the system and their own rules for what was right and wrong in a group. For example, as part of our 'exploring prejudice' exercise, we asked the group, "What's something you always wanted to know about another race/culture/gender, but didn't like to ask?" The participants put their questions anonymously in a hat, the facilitator picked them out at random, read them out and then the group would answer them as best they could. Some examples were:

- Why do Muslims spit in the street during Ramadan?
- Why do white people wash all their dishes in the same bowl of dirty water?
- Why do some women not shave their hairy armpits?

Our job was to facilitate the discussions and ensure everyone had a voice. I watched one of our trainee facilitators take a question from the hat, read it and crumple it up and throw it on the floor. I picked it up and said to the group that I'd noticed she'd censored a question.

Dawn: It's not appropriate for this setting.

Caitlin: **Can I just check … Someone's put this question into the hat and Dawn thinks it's inappropriate to read it out so she's thrown it away. What are your thoughts?**

There was a ripple in the group. Some thought it was outrageous to have their questions censored. Some thought it didn't matter and she'd probably know best, but generally the agreement was that if the question went in the hat, it wasn't up to the facilitator to act as censor. Dawn said she still wasn't prepared to read it so I read the question.

Caitlin: **Why don't black men give head?**

I asked the group, including Dawn, what they thought of the question. She said that she felt it was inappropriate and unfitting for a workplace course because people were compelled to attend these trainings and shouldn't be subjected to sexually explicit sentences. Others said that since someone had asked the question they had a right to be answered same as everybody else. Someone else said that it wasn't a sensible question anyway because in his experience they did. Then the group agreed that it wasn't relevant to getting work and those who wanted to discuss it could do so in the break time and they let it go.

While Dawn had decided that talking about private sex acts was unsuitable for a work place, the decision to put that question in the hat might be the same kind of decision that was contributing to that client being out of work. If the group thought it was inappropriate, I felt that one of them needed to say so and the person who put it in needed to hear the group say that it was out of order.

> If the group thought it was inappropriate, I felt that one of them needed to say so and the person whose question it was needed to hear the group say that it was out of order.

If Dawn took the question out then she was rescuing the group from one of its own members and assuming they weren't taking care of themselves.

By reading the question out, regardless of whether I thought it was appropriate or not, I was making space for the group members to use their own voices to feedback to one another. I was assuming that the group could take responsibility for what was happening in the moment which I hoped, in turn, would lead to a greater sense of agency and more action. An alternative would have been for Dawn to have read the question to herself and then to have told the group she didn't feel able to read it out loud and to have asked them what they wanted to have happen. At the time I was trying out different principles, sticking with them and finding out what effect they had.

Was It Worth It?

Once the courses were running regularly and the advisors were managing their caseloads, we needed to start evaluating how successful the approach was. In a target-driven environment there is no shortage of external measurements; however it wasn't easy to separate how much of the shift in job outcomes was down to this particular systemic way of working or whether it was just down to the attitudes of these high performing advisors or to the nice new offices.

We do know that prior to this W2W company taking over the case loads from this borough, the average number of people in this area using Welfare to Work agencies who found work was between 25% and 30% and of those 25%-30% only 40% of them still had that job three months after they got it. This meant that 60% of all of those people who did get a job came back onto the books of the agencies, with the attendant costs in time and money and the corresponding despondency.

Following the recruitment and training of this staff team with Richard, the average number of people coming into this company who found work was 50%. Much more importantly for us, 80% of these people were still in that work three months later. We felt that this indicated a real shift from people being forced into work they didn't want in order to allow an industry to hit its targets, to groups of people finding sustainable work that suited them.

We continued supporting the company for a few months with fresh recruitment drives and specific modelling projects. For example, at one time they wanted us to uncover how it was that some advisors hit their high job-outcome targets without getting over stressed while others burned out or fell below the acceptable target. We were able to come in and cleanly model some examples of excellence and we uncovered three factors that were making a difference: always taking a lunch break; having a prioritisation system to stream clients; and not working late more than once a week. Once they knew that these were the important factors they could make new policies or encourage people to take their lunch breaks. We weren't needed for this part of the exercise. After a short space of time the in-house trainers were independent of us and able to recruit, induct and train their clients and colleagues themselves.

I think many things about this project were exemplary, including the rigour in our recruitment process and the congruence in taking staff through the same process that they would ask their long term unemployed clients to go through. This was the first time we'd run such an ambitious and long-term programme and there were inevitably lots of learnings that came out of it further on in the future.

Cautionary Tale

I had hoped that once we left the company and it expanded and grew across the UK that Clean Language and our Systemic Modelling™ approach would underpin everything they did. Instead, after a couple of years, they kept some processes, forgot some principles and in some areas it became so dilute as to be undetectable.

One factor was that the six internal trainers were all at the level of advisor rather than manager and had no control over high level training and recruitment decisions. When, a few years down the line, the company expanded, some new senior managers decided that advisors only had to complete three days of the client training course instead of the full ten and the internal trainers didn't have the power to challenge this decision. This meant that future advisors could no longer tell their clients that they'd attended the course themselves and they were lacking in the rigorous self-reflection the course provided.

I would proceed with more caution in who I chose as an in-house trainer in future. If they were going to be the internal champions for the approach, they needed to be from a range of different positions through the company so that they have as wide a sphere of influence as possible.

CHAPTER 6

Getting Too Big For My Boots

*Working with a secondary school
to improve the learning culture*

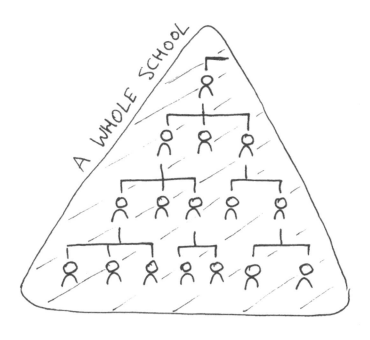

As the W2W project was coming to an end, and before I knew how sustainable the processes would be, new pieces of work were coming in. I was invited to design a 'clean' training for the police to interview vulnerable or very young witnesses. I was asked to provide clean mediation to senior managers in crisis to prevent issues ending up in court. I was brought in to international teams who needed shared metaphors to mediate across their cultural diversity. I was on a roll and felt as though I could tackle anything.

I went on an awayday with Nancy to think about where I wanted the company to go next. As we walked together across Hadrian's Wall, Nancy helped me to clarify my outcomes and I helped her to clarify hers.

I had a vision of working with a whole community; I wanted community leaders involved so that the change would start at the top. I'd need a group of movers and shakers who would be my champions in the community, and then a whole organisation as a pilot. I wanted to investigate the power of 'it', which was what I called Systemic Modelling™ at that time as I hadn't quite settled on a name for it then. I also wanted to work with Nancy to set up some more robust ways of tracking and measuring what was actually happening.

Then, as if by magic, the phone rang. It was the CEO of a community change agency who had access to European Regeneration funding and wanted innovative interventions to help regenerate her city. She had heard of my work from a number of sources and wanted me to deliver a range of projects. The serendipity was extraordinary.

I travelled to meet her, shared my whole community vision, and she went about finding contacts within the city council to run a mini Metaphors at Work project with the heads of all of the departments. She set up a meeting to inspire movers and shakers across the city to join us, including a meeting with the head of education who agreed that we could work with a whole school. Nancy started investigating how we could track the changes and report back to the funders.

The timescales were very tight and the agency set about finding a whole secondary school for us to work with even before I'd done the work with the city council. The education department was concerned about other schools knowing about the project and getting argumentative or competitive, so one was quietly chosen for us. This meant I didn't know the head teacher and I hadn't done any Clean Scoping with them. The staff didn't know us and hadn't invited us in to help them and I had no idea what kind of system we were going into. Alarm bells should have been ringing for me, but I was so excited at the thought of a big

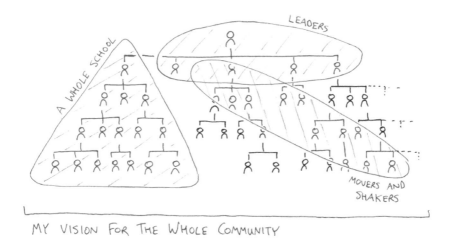

MY VISION FOR THE WHOLE COMMUNITY

juicy project, which included funding for Nancy to evaluate it properly, that I was all action and no reflection.

Since I didn't have any people to model, I was designing the project based on past results. In my mind I thought we'd facilitate the Senior Management Team (SMT) at the school with a Metaphors at Work approach. They'd love it and champion it to the staff and we'd go on to teach the staff to use clean questions in the classroom. We'd offer one-to-one coaching to staff and children, model best practice in the school and help staff to learn effectively from one another. The young people and staff would soon become a self-modelling learning community and their school would become a world class teaching and learning institute.

This was working so well in my mind that I started inviting people to come and deliver on these imaginary interventions. I invited trained Systemic Modellers to run the group facilitation and leading Symbolic Modellers to deliver the one-to-one work. All this while we were still writing up the imagined project plan to get sign-off on the funding.

In retrospect, I'd really gotten way too big for my boots. I knew nothing about project management on this scale and didn't have the experience to know what I didn't know. Prior to this, my project sponsors had been internal to their companies and had managed all the administration, finance and HR issues. Now I was inviting a whole load of associates to take part in an unspecified project, with many different strands and an unknown client, to run a process I still couldn't articulate and that most of them didn't fully understand.

But this was my chance: to make right what I'd got wrong with the youth project; to help create a modelling context across a whole school rather than just with the kids; and to transform a city and show the world what we could do. So I pressed on regardless and started assembling the team.

The whole project was suffering from the starting point of the sponsor bringing in an outside agency to change a school: X brings in Y because they want Z to change. It was the opposite of the work I'd been developing so far which was all about careful, iterative change that ensured that those with the greatest sphere of influence were the ones who were willing to change their behaviour first and test the processes before inflicting them on everybody else. The city council were already in special measures and had all kinds of external agencies around. The school had so many change programmes running it was suffering from 'initiativitis'. We were just one more uninvited voice telling people to do things differently.

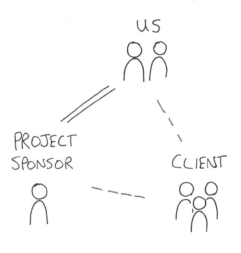

The Systemic Modelling™ principles that had guided us in earlier projects were being broken right, left and centre:

- **The change processes should be led by the most influential points in the system.** The project sponsor who booked us had no influence over the leaders in the city council and the head of education had no interest in the whole school project. There would be absolutely no leading from the top in this project.
- **The motivation for change must come from and be sustained from within the system.** There was no motivation from the leaders in the school to engage in the project. The CEO might want the school to change to justify her funding

> The motivation for change must come from and be sustained from within the system.

choices. I might want the school to change to rectify mistakes I'd made earlier in my career. The European Regeneration funders might want the kids to get better results and to find sustainable employment BUT no one in the school had invited us in. The school hadn't indicated any desire to change.

- **All those asking others to change should be demonstrating that change themselves.** There was no leader in the school demonstrating by example that the process was useful. This was a basic rule of Systemic Modelling™: that whoever booked us would start using the tools from Clean Scoping onwards and would be able to demonstrate to colleagues how useful the tools were before they brought us into the wider system. In this project, the school leadership team gave the project the go ahead with no idea what they were agreeing to. About two weeks into the project, the head declined to take part in any more of the sessions, didn't champion the project with her staff and didn't agree to those who were interested taking time out to attend training.

> All those asking others to change should be demonstrating that change themselves.

- **The clients should invest their own resources in creating the change.** The school wasn't paying for the modelling or the coaching sessions and there were no consequences if they wasted this resource. If staff didn't turn up when they'd agreed to and wasted our time, that was our issue not theirs. The project sponsor was outside of the system so the spheres of influence weren't aligned. We had nothing to hold the client accountable for.

- **All change processes should be incremental so that the facilitator and the system can learn as they go along.** The time limits for designing and delivering the project were really tight. Between the initial meeting where the management team agreed to take us on and a couple of weeks later when the head declined to take part, we'd already completed our observations of the school and the SMT and invited our colleagues to come and start coaching. There wasn't time or money to find another school. We were stuck with the path we'd agreed to regardless of how it was going. We couldn't use all of the emergent information available.

It was a dog's breakfast before we started. I'd love to say that this was as obvious at the time as it is in retrospect but I was far too busy planning, scheming, delivering, moving my family to the city and getting ready to triumph.

This haphazard setup did, however, give us an evaluation opportunity we'd been wanting for ages: we were able to go into the school and observe the behaviours of staff and students before any Clean Scoping had happened and before they'd started changing their behaviour. In the past there was a lot of Clean Scoping and a lot of learning and development before we ever signed a contract which meant any measurements we did were of people already in the process of change.

With this new opportunity, we could run a base-line assessment before we started. Nancy and I considered what behaviours we should be looking for, what changes we were likely to see and also how the observers could be open to changes that we couldn't even think of at this stage. I had a list of the kinds of behaviour changes I'd seen in past projects. A contact from Yale University helped us think through the project from a child development perspective. And Nancy considered what kinds of behaviours would be indicative of positive learning environments. We decided to go into the classrooms and look for:

- Number of closed questions asked by teacher.
- Number of open questions asked by teacher.
- Percentage of class time spent on teacher-led whole class teaching.
- Percentage of time spent on small group collaborative learning.
- Incidents of positive feedback.
- Incidents of negative feedback.
- Number of times pupil answers teacher's question.
- Number of times teacher answers own question.

We would use a tally system each time one of these behaviours was demonstrated. As well as counting specific classroom behaviours, the observers would spend time in corridors and classrooms and record behaviours over a set period of time.

The Flower Model came into its own. The observers needed to be able to distinguish what they were seeing and hearing from the inferences they were making about them. They needed to know some of their own patterns and some of the differences between them to ensure a consistency in their observations. They not only needed to know what patterns they were observing for; they also had to have their attention open to other patterns we might not have thought of.

I designed an observation and feedback process for the SMT so that I could create a model of their behaviours and the dynamics in the group.

The evaluation team set off towards the classrooms and corridors with Nancy while I went with James Lawley to observe the SMT meetings in action.

We were taken aback by the school culture. I'd worked in some of the most deprived areas of London, with some of the most disadvantaged people, but nothing prepared me for what we found at this school. Here are a handful of the observations from our teams:

- On arriving at school, students were throwing snowballs at staff and at us – and not in a playful way.
- When James and I walked into the SMT meeting, we sat down and no one asked who we were or what we wanted. We had to introduce ourselves and no one paid any attention. It was as though anyone could just wander in and out at will.
- The staff showing us round walked into classrooms without knocking, spoke over the teachers and talked to us about the teachers and kids as though they weren't there.
- In a top maths class we observed a student standing on the table while others went through the store cupboard and handed him text books which he threw out of the window.
- In the same class two students were simulating oral sex behind the teacher's head while another filmed it on their mobile phone.
- In a science lesson the students set fire to wooden splints that the science teacher was holding behind his back.
- In the same lesson a group of students wrapped another boy in tape, binding his hands, feet and mouth and then rolled him off the desk.
- Students regularly ran, shoved, pushed and punched as they moved around the school and our staff often felt unsafe in the corridors.
- We witnessed one female student repeatedly punching another over the shoulder of the Head of Geography while members of staff walked past.
- In one corridor we met a teacher who had locked her students in the classroom and who was standing in tears refusing to let them out unless a senior member of staff came to her aid.
- Although there was a behaviour policy it was enforced differently in each classroom which meant that any teacher trying to send a student to

detention might spend 15 minutes arguing about whether or not this was fair.

Despite these appalling behaviours there'd only been two fixed-term exclusions that year.

The playgrounds were even worse:

- All the toilets were locked because of past issues with water fights, so students didn't have access to drinking water and couldn't go to the toilet unless the playground supervisors unlocked the door.
- The staff on duty were constantly locking and unlocking the toilets in the corridors all through the breaks, which meant that they weren't available to observe or intervene with playground dynamics.
- The children had free access to flavoured fizzy water, full of aspartame, which they got in plastic bottles. The fields were littered with bottle tops which meant that the first part of each sports lesson was wasted as kids cleared the pitch of bottle tops.

And when we observed the SMT we noticed huge inconsistencies in their communication:

- The head said she wanted staff to be self-motivated and to work on their own initiative. In the same meeting when she heard that someone had done something without her permission she glared at them and asked why they hadn't agreed it with her first.
- One school leader was trying to encourage collaboration between the pupils through a house system, dividing each form into four houses and creating inter-house competitions. In the same meeting a different school leader was setting up competitions between forms in order to achieve the same purpose. Pupils were often invited to two meetings in one day and no one knew whether to have allegiance to their form or their house.

From a Triune Brain perspective the staff and the students were all operating under inconsistent rules and could never settle their mammalian brains. We guessed that the inconsistency, noise, confusion and the lack of water meant that most people, staff and students, spent most of their days in the reptilian state of of fight, flight or freeze. It was exhausting just visiting.

As long as I'm patient, I can help most clients to separate their problems into evidence and interpretation. I can also help them to think about what they'd like to have happen instead and facilitate them to develop metaphor models for their outcomes as part of the Clean Scoping.

Almost every interview and coaching session with the school leaders had a strong problem focus and it was particularly difficult to get anyone to shift their attention towards how things could change:

- We'd love to improve our kids' grades but we're like a sausage factory. You can't expect fine sausages from low grade meat.
- The head is inconsistent, so we're inconsistent, so the kids don't know if they're coming or going. No one could teach well in this environment.
- Most of these children come from backgrounds where their parents don't have a real interest in their education. We can't expect them to engage fully in education; they're doing the best they can.
- Yes, lots of the kids are out of control and the teachers can't manage them. I keep a whole group of the 'unusuals' in my own classroom so that the staff have a chance of managing the others.

This pattern came from the pupils as well as the teachers:

- The teachers here can't control the kids and if they aren't going to behave why should I?
- I really want to work and get my exams but I just can't. Even if I try to work at the back the other kids make fun of me and steal my books.

I couldn't find a way of using clean questions or the Karma Cycle to help them develop a balanced landscape of what *was* working as well as what *wasn't* working for them. In this organisation there didn't seem to be any attention on what people wanted, on possibilities or things they could aim for.

One day, near the start of this project, I was having my hair cut and I heard on the radio that the city football team had had a really good season. I commented on this to the hairdresser, who said, "Yes but it won't last, it will only get everyone's hopes up and then we'll be disappointed." It was a city-wide virus of disappointment, blame, dashed hopes and lethargy.

One of our fellow clean modellers, Michael Mallows, saw my bafflement with this pattern. To help me and my team understand what was happening, he introduced a model to categorise the statements we were hearing as being 'drama' statements. This was my first introduction to Stephen Karpman's 'Drama Triangle'. This model comes from the field of Transactional Analysis and essentially it proposes that when people aren't getting what they want, they often move to one of three positions of contempt or not being OK:

Persecutor: Someone or something else is at fault.

- You aren't OK as you are.
- They need to change.
- You aren't good enough.
- You should know better.
- They're lazy, dangerous, stupid, incompetent ...

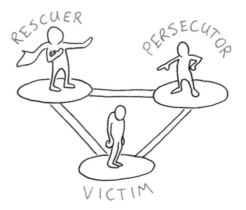

Rescuer: Someone else isn't good enough and I have to cover for them.

- I'm OK as I am, but you or they aren't OK, so I need to help.
- Let me do this for you.
- She can't be trusted so I have to ...
- He's unable to ... so I do it instead.

This position usually leads to the rescuer moving to persecutor or victim over time.

Victim: It's me, my school, my city who isn't good enough.

- I'm not OK as I am.
- I'm unable to ...
- Life's unfair.
- We don't stand a chance.
- I can't ...
- It's alright for you but we can't ...

The issue with all three drama positions is that people believe that their situation can't change unless some external force changes it. When they are on the Drama Triangle people give up a sense of responsibility and wallow in the drama. This is the opposite of inspiring capability and seemed to be inspiring futility.

Here we had a whole school, within a city, with a press and leaders in the city council all telling the same stories, over and over again about how things were inevitably bad and couldn't change.

I realise, looking back, that I had been incredibly lucky with the projects I'd run before. They had visionary leaders who were confident that the world could be other than it was and had the courage and conviction to try out new ways of making things happen.

Also, in past projects, if my Clean Scoping process revealed that the person who had called me in didn't have that vision and I hadn't been able to get a clear, balanced model of what they wanted and what they were going to do to achieve it, I just didn't take on the work.

Now I'd taken on the work without any meaningful scoping, invited a bunch of colleagues to help deliver the project, signed a contract to say that we would deliver, only to find out that there wasn't an outcome in sight.

From Drama to Karma

Once Michael explained the Drama Triangle clearly, I could see how it related to our work. David Grove's approach when working one-to-one with his clients helped to name and then resolve their internal dramas and helped them to move towards learning, insight and fresh outcomes. In his footsteps I'd developed a series of models and processes that attempted to do the same thing at a group level.

I could review past projects using the Drama Triangle to reflect on them. The original contract for the youth project had been for me to get the young people to manage their tempers and learn to read. This would have meant coming from a rescuing position where I was OK, the kids weren't and I would make them OK. The Software company was generally low on drama and that's what had made it so easy to work with. Diversity Training was often done from a position of persecution with minorities being seen as the victims. The Welfare to Work industry is rife with drama and advisors regularly either persecute or rescue the unemployed – and the kinds of courses they force people to go on create more of a sense of victim-hood and despondency.

The approach I'd been developing encouraged the system to model itself and it trusted that change would emerge with less drama and with a stronger outcome focus as they paid exquisite attention to themselves and one another. The whole approach was about moving away from Drama and towards Karma.

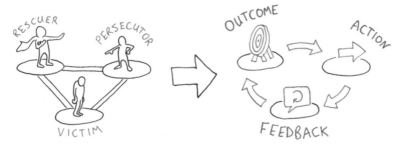

I was absolutely delighted with Michael's insight and having the Drama Triangle to hand made it much easier to give meaningful feedback to the group about their attitude and how the very way they were thinking about themselves and the kids was a major part of the problem. So, where to start with a school that didn't have any motivation to change and who didn't really want us there? We wandered around detecting Drama and encouraging people to move towards Karma.

- We gave feedback to the head about how she was giving one message of empowerment in words, and then undermining it with actions - and offered her coaching. (She declined.)
- We met with the SMT, shared our observations of what was happening in the classrooms and corridors and asked them what they'd like to have happen.

- We offered one-to-one observation and coaching to the deputy head and to the assistant deputy head, who had both agreed to coordinate the project.
- We ran a whole school awayday called 'Shift Happens' to get staff to understand the Drama Triangle and to consider what outcomes they might have for themselves, their students and the school. We encouraged them to use Clean Feedback and to think systemically about what was working well and not so well in the school and what they'd like to have happen to work at their best there.
- We'd noticed that a handful of teachers *were* able to keep order and their classrooms had a completely different culture to the rest of the school. So we offered to model what they were doing differently, record their classrooms and shared this as a staff training resource.
- We offered one-to-one clean coaching to any member of staff or pupil who asked for it.
- We taught Systemic Modelling™ skills as part of the drama curriculum to the 11-, 12- and 13-year-olds to give them a chance to learn self-awareness and collaborative learning.
- We offered one-to-one clean coaching to 14- and 15-year-old pupils who were borderline between getting a grade C or a grade D to boost their results.
- We offered 12- and 13-year-old pupils a peer mentoring project using Systemic Modelling™ tools and encouraged them to become peer mentors to the following year's new intake of children
- We ran 'modelling temper' sessions for pupils who were excluded from class for violence
- We offered classes in Magical Spelling®, a model for spelling English visually and for taking responsibility for your own learning state.

We did many little things to prime the system and the individuals in it to reflect on their patterns, develop their outcomes and collaborate to achieve them. We had no real sense of direction and there was no one within the school pulling the threads together. While we kept on modelling and feeding back and asking what people would like to have happen, it didn't feel like we were creating a strong network of attention. It felt more like emptying all the ingredients I could find in my kitchen into one bowl and hoping it would miraculously turn into a cake.

We were all very busy trying things out, getting frustrated, getting together at the end of the day, giving feedback and setting new outcomes for the next day. We all learned a lot about practising our skills and staying curious, even in crisis, but I was very unsure how useful we were being in the school. A big problem was that we were getting caught up in the school's patterns and focussing more and more on the detail. We weren't opening out our attention and fully facing current reality and the 'awfulness' of the situation. In short, we weren't applying our clean modelling principles to the daily problems and to ourselves. This became part of our group's game. We all became involved in self-deception and found ways to avoid bringing what was happening overall out into the open.

> We weren't opening out our attention and fully facing current reality and the 'awfulness' of the situation.

Shift Happens

My leadership of this project was awful, shameful even and certainly not an example of the standards I'd set so far in Training Attention. In hindsight I'm amazed that anything changed at all.

But, miraculously, shift did begin to happen. The first big change was with the deputy head. I'd been observing him in meetings, in the corridors and in his classroom and had noticed some interesting patterns that fit into the Drama Triangle.

One day, during a meeting to discuss the project, a child ran past his door in tears. The deputy called him in to ask him what was wrong and the child said he'd been sent out of lesson and put in detention because he was late but that the teacher hadn't given him an opportunity to explain that he was late because he'd been helping another teacher carry books. The deputy abandoned his meeting with me and took the child's hand saying, while striding down the corridor, "Well don't you worry about a thing. I'll go and see Miss right now and she'll have to listen if I'm with you." He strode into her classroom and told the teacher she had to let the pupil back into the lesson. There were similar incidents with teachers where they would knock on his door and say a class was out of control and he would dash off down the corridor to berate the class, get them in order and then take the class until the next bell.

On top of this he ran classes for a group he called the 'unusuals' – students who were so disruptive in other classes that he felt it was safer for them to stay in his room. This meant he was using teaching time every day looking after these students on top of his other strategic duties.

With the Drama Triangle as a reflection tool, he could see that he was operating from a rescuer position. Sometimes he was persecuting teachers and making victims of the kids, other times he was persecuting the kids and rescuing the teachers. He recognised how this undermined and dis-empowered his staff and the students and left them feeling less able to deal with the situation next time. Once we started, he could see example after example of what he was doing that he thought of as helpful but actually escalated the situations.

He was courageous in the face of this feedback and immediately asked for support from his closest colleagues, as well as from us, to change his patterns. We coached him as he set an outcome to be more centred in his response to issues when they arose and to ask both staff and students what they would like to have happen and how he could support them to resolve their differences themselves.

When he felt the urge to rescue he would ask Clean Feedback questions to clarify the situation and to remind himself not to slip into premature evaluation and drama. He brought this to the attention of his assistant deputy and she agreed to give him a signal every time he moved to rescuer and drama. He would stop himself and endeavour to move to facilitator instead.

The most immediate effect was that the staff and students were taken aback when he wouldn't come to their aid or fight their fights. It took a couple of months before they learned that he was serious. At first distressed staff and students sought out the assistant deputy instead and this really didn't suit her. With the Drama Triangle in mind, she mirrored the deputy and asked teachers what they wanted to have happen, what they were going to do about it and how she could support them. She made it clear that she wouldn't rescue the situation for them.

Both the deputy and assistant deputy got into the habit of asking staff and students clean questions and getting them to separate evidence from inference so that conversations went more like this:

Student: Miss, Sir just threw me out when I wasn't even talking.
Asst. Deputy: **And what would you like to have happen?**
Student: I want you to sort it out miss.

Asst. Deputy: **What happened just before he threw you out?**
Student: He was going on at me.
Asst. Deputy: **What did you see or hear that you call going on at you?**
Student: Well he was asking me to answer a question from the book.
Asst. Deputy: **And what was happening for you when** he was asking you to answer a question?
Student: I was listening to Robbo tell me about football and I can't do two things at once.
Asst. Deputy: **And** he was asking you to answer a question **and** you were listening to Robbo, **and then what happened?**
Student: Then he said if I didn't want to learn I might as well leave. *(Student is visibly calmer now.)*
Asst. Deputy: **OK, so what would you like to have happen now?**
Student: I want to go back to my lesson.
Asst. Deputy: **What needs to happen before you can** go back to your lesson?
Student: I could say sorry.
Asst. Deputy: **And can you try that now?**
Student: OK.

Now we had two leaders who were making use of the processes and demonstrating how to use them practically. But they were only two in an organisation of 1800. What about the rest of the school?

The next big shift was a new idea that emerged from one of our debrief sessions at the end of a long day. There were a few staff who had really taken to the project and the processes – some senior managers, some teachers, some classroom assistants – and between them they knew the school from a number of perspectives. They also included two advanced skills teachers who had a special remit to observe and offer coaching to the rest of the staff body.

We invited all nine of them to come together and offered them full training in Systemic Modelling™ including all the basic models and how to use them in classroom observation and peer coaching. They became a mini-learning community and once they'd learned the models, they started observing one another at work, giving one another feedback and learning from one another's expertise. Like the children in the youth project they began modelling one another on themes like teaching at their best, making decision, staying calm etc.

This group called themselves 'super coaches' and started using the processes in all their interactions. They became adept at unpacking drama and turning it into action. In staff meetings, if a colleague was going into drama about an issue, one of the super coaches would interrupt and ask, "So when that's an issue, what would you like to have happen?" They also they intervened in altercations and facilitated staff and students to come to joint outcomes.

About four weeks into this project they told us how differently they were acting and what a difference that was making to the way they felt at school.

- Things are a lot calmer, so the kids are a lot calmer.
- I can separate their (the kids') behaviour from their identity.
- There's a split second where I can think more clearly in my head. I feel the rise of anger but I know that shouting won't get me what I want.
- I now hold back from doing things for the kids and I'm more likely to let them do it themselves.
- I feel I really do know my patterns now, some I didn't even know I had.
- I've realised that I revel in rescuing and I almost go looking for it. I'm trying not to do that now.
- Clean Language makes me shut up, listen and ask clarification questions. I babble less.
- I'm now giving feedback in the same, straightforward way whether it's negative or positive; I say: This is what I've seen, this is what I interpret, what support would you like from me?

Unfortunately, this training of the super coaches coincided with the last six weeks of the project and our training sessions were frequently double-booked with other staff meetings which meant we were wasting at least 50% of our time and resources. At this stage we had no evidence that these embryonic changes would continue into the next term.

Our project ended, we packed up and left. We had done everything we'd agreed to do in our contract. We'd always known it was experimental and that it may or may not work but I think every one of us left the city feeling quite dejected.

Nine Months Later

Nine months later we fulfilled our evaluation promise and went back to the school to see what, if anything, had changed. We walked down the corridors, sat in SMT meetings, and classrooms and completed our observation sheets. We interviewed staff and students and analysed their answers.

Even before we started our observations... Just walking into the school... What a difference! I'm not suggesting it was a perfect learning environment but it was nothing like it had been a year before:

- In the corridors the students walked at a reasonable pace rather than running, shoving or punching.
- Although students often talked loudly there was no screaming or name calling.
- Classrooms were orderly, with teachers teaching and students working together, often in small groups.
- Pupils put their hands up, answered questions and appeared to be engaged in their lessons.
- When I arrived at the SMT meeting I was formally introduced to new staff members and asked what I wanted from the meeting, what I was recording and what I would do with the results. It was no longer possible to wander around wherever I felt like. There were boundaries.
- The super coaches had transformed into a behavioural management group and were ensuring that all interventions and new policies were well thought through and communicated clearly to all staff.
- The disciplinary process was now simple, clear and enforced consistently.

- There had been 83 suspensions and one exclusion; a rise from 2 to 83. Now a massive rise in suspensions might seem like a negative result but for us it indicated a huge shift in the teachers' ability to control the pupils and create meaningful consequences for them.
- The number of pupils achieving five A-C grades had risen from 23% to 43%.

I caught up with a few of the students from our drama classes to ask whether there'd been any changes in the school since I'd last seen them.

Student A: Oh yeah, we used to just shout out all the time, but now when you want to say something, you put your hand up. And then the teacher comes to you.

Student B: Yeah, remember before if somebody gave an answer, and it was wrong, we all took the piss out of them. But now, if someone gets it wrong, we explain why it's wrong, and then we help each other.

It was almost as if they had no idea how this had happened. There weren't just changes in pupils' perceptions. After the classroom observations, Nancy analysed the observational sheets and noticed a remarkable shift. Prior to the project, observers had recorded that an average of 73% of the questions teachers asked were closed and could only be answered with a 'yes' or a 'no'. I'd called this teaching method 'guess the answer in my head' because all the attention was on getting a single answer right. Teachers almost never asked a question to which they didn't already have an answer. They rarely asked for opinions, personal experiences or creativity. Nine months later the number of closed questions had fallen to 25%. Now, on average, 75% of the questions asked by teachers were open and were being answered by the pupils. This seemed to indicate that both pupils and teachers were more engaged in the learning process.

I think the most exciting result was that all of these behavioural changes were just as significant for teachers and pupils with whom we hadn't worked directly. This indicated to us that the changes had become 'the way things are done around here'. We'd discovered that it was possible to create systemic culture change

> The behavioural changes were just as significant for teachers and pupils with whom we hadn't worked directly.

by changing the culture across a few influential people without having to train everyone in the system. We'd reached that elusive tipping point and the school had shifted from being in constant Drama to being able to apply the Karma Cycle; not formally, but conversationally and without even consciously thinking about it. It felt like a glimmer of success.

With everything else that was happening in the city and in the school, of course it isn't possible to put a cause and effect to the results we observed but it was an encouraging indication that we might find more cost effective ways of effecting large scale culture change in the future.

Cautionary Tale

In many ways this whole project is a cautionary tale about getting too big for your boots and developing a sense of confidence that far outstrips your competence.

The results were unexpectedly good but, with greater diligence, I believe we could have achieved the same kinds of change in a much shorter time and at a fraction of the cost. It was a poor use of public funding and it made me determined to approach any future projects with greater humility, clearer boundaries and a lot more caution from the very start.

CHAPTER 7

Inspiring Capability

*Enhancing the staff and student experience
in higher education*

After the school experience I retreated for a little while to have a big think about what I had done and not done and what I would do differently as a result. I was keener than ever to work with larger systems but I'd learned my lesson about project sponsors and spheres of influence and now set out to find a fresh piece of work that I could set up with more caution and due diligence.

Just when I needed some help with this quest, I was lucky enough to meet up with Sarah Smith, another of those serendipitous meetings in the journey of Systemic Modelling™. Sarah is a systemic thinker and networker from Merseyside in the North of England and like so many of my northern mentors including Chris Grimsley, Glenda Sutcliffe and Cricket Kemp, Sarah's attention was on quietly creating the inspirational networks that help to transform communities, not on her own ego. She was skilfully bringing together 'movers and shakers' across Merseyside and supporting new thinking and emergent knowledge.

Sarah invited me to one of her groups to run the Five Senses exercise and to share examples of my past work to see if anyone was interested. One member of the group was scowling throughout the exercise and the more attention I gave her the more she scowled – I had inferred that she hated what she was hearing but it turns out that that is just the face she pulls when she's having a big idea.

This is the story of how her big idea led to a wonderful project that used every aspect of Systemic Modelling™, was a joy to design and deliver, was sustainable and is still running years after I've left.

Modelling Excellence in Teaching and Learning in Higher Education

The scowler unexpectedly called the next day, said her name was Sarah and that she was from a local university. "Our department has just been awarded a Centre of Excellence in Teaching and Learning (CETL) which means we have funds for developing and disseminating excellence across three university faculties. Would you come in and talk to us about some of your work? We're thinking of asking you to give us a two-hour workshop on creative ways of thinking."

Although I knew I wouldn't blindly agree to do what she wanted, I agreed to meet her. When I got to the university, we started Clean Scoping for the two-hour workshop she had in mind, then about the wider project, her outcomes, expectations, hopes and concerns. The conversation went something like this:

Sarah: Could you come onto our awayday and do a session on creative thinking to help facilitate the staff to talk to one another?

Caitlin: **What would you like to have happen during that workshop?**

Sarah: I want them to see that we're not on the same page and then talk properly about what we're going to do together.

Caitlin: **What will they be doing or saying as they** talk properly?

Sarah: Being honest, challenging each other.

Caitlin: **What's it like at the moment?**

Sarah: Well, the other two departments are both up their own arses. We'll end up doing all of the work and they'll take all the credit.

Caitlin: **And when** they're up their own arses, **what do they do or say that's an example of that?**

Why Did Sarah Make That Call?

"I had been worrying that the CETL project would just be another talking shop where nothing actually happened. I wanted it to be action-orientated and of real benefit for the students. Once I came across your work, I began to see a way of creating something genuinely impactful.

"I was already using goal-setting to help my students develop their learning skills and their Personal Development Profiles (PDP) and I knew I was scratching the surface of what was possible but I didn't know any other way of doing it.

"When we did the Five Senses exercise, I realized that there were so many different ways of understanding one concept, it was incredible. It still fascinates me now. Then, times my learning by 300 students. It was all about people knowing themselves more and understanding others. If Personal Development Planning was to be successful, we had to create something that allowed the students to become a learning community.

"I also had an idea about bringing the Five Senses exercise into the university team who were managing the project. I felt if Caitlin could help them see that we weren't on the same page then we could do something about it before the project went any further."

Whenever I hear contempt like this, I immediately start paying attention. It seemed unlikely that her colleagues perceived themselves as 'up their own arses'. So I wondered what she'd seen and heard to say this. (On reflection she says they weren't actually up their own arses, it's just that she was taking a drama position, thinking about all of the things that might go wrong and already blaming them for things she imagined they might do.)

Sarah: They're more interested in their research than in students. I'm worried that the students won't get anything from the project. *(I note that Sarah values students more than research.)*

Caitlin: **What specific, measurable shifts would you be looking for to show that the CETL project was a success and of benefit to the students?** *(Asking for evidence.)*

Sarah: We'd increase student retention and see more of them through to completion. I'd see students working together to improve their results. The students would be relying less on their tutors and more on small learning communities and networks that they built up between themselves.

Caitlin: **What kind of** small learning communities?

Sarah: In their tutorial groups, they'll give each other feedback, challenge each other, inspire each other.

Caitlin: **And before** they challenge each other … **what happens before that?**

Sarah: They'll need to know each other better and trust each other. *(Context for change.)*

Caitlin: **And they'll** know each other, trust each other, challenge and give feedback. **Is there anything else?**

Sarah: Students will start making the connections between one set of lectures and another and get an overall sense of how the different lecture series fit together.

Caitlin: **What would need to have happened for** them to make connections **like this?** *(Context for change)*

I was back in my groove. I had no idea what the client really wanted and very little idea of what I might offer her. I had an expectation that I probably wouldn't give her what she first asked for because I thought the chances of her already having worked out what she needed from a systemic perspective were quite small.

As Sarah was talking, I was not really listening to her in the ordinary sense. I was listening to the pattern of the way that she was talking. I was listening for who she was holding in contempt, what was driving her and what were her highest values. I was noticing how wide, or narrow, her sphere of attention was and what she wasn't thinking about. I was using questions from the Karma Cycle to build up her model of what was happening, what she wanted to have happen and what needed to happen next. The CETL project involved two other departments so in my own mental model I made a space for the two other leaders who may or may not be involved. I needed to know the limits of the system I'd be working in so as to make the change sustainable within that part of the system.

I wanted Sarah's attention to be on what needed to happen before she could have what she wanted. I asked whether the staff gave one another feedback or made connections across one another's lecture series. Sarah laughed and said, "No, absolutely not." I asked what stopped them. She said there was a lack of mutual understanding and respect. Smaller issues went unspoken, festered and remained unresolved. She mentioned a lack of time and a fear of the response they might get if they gave feedback.

I asked what would have to be different in the staff team so that they could behave in a way that demonstrated what they wanted from their students and Sarah said they'd need to know each other well, trust each other – and she didn't think they'd be able to shift. As I helped her to build a broader model, it became clear to her that the shift needed to be with the staff and potentially with the management before we addressed the student culture – and that was just in Sarah's department, never mind the other two departments involved in the project.

A couple of hours on an awayday weren't going to be enough to create a significant shift in the thinking and behaviour of these three departments. At this stage I didn't know what was possible but I knew I definitely wouldn't do the two-hour session Sarah had initially proposed.

Instead, I offered, "What if I facilitate just you and the other two leaders of the project through a live meeting on something important, get the three of you thinking the way I've just worked with you today. You don't need to pay me, but if that facilitated meeting means that the three of you are able to work more effectively to lead the project, would you then be able to put a business case through for having me run the whole of the awayday with some preparation beforehand?"

I reasoned with Sarah that this way she'd have access to my services for nothing and if I was rubbish in the small group than she wouldn't have embarrassed herself by bringing in a poor external facilitator to the wider group. If I was useful in the small group then she'd be confident to explain why I should run the whole day. For me, this plan gave me possible access to the whole of the system for the whole day and more time to work out if this could be the next big project for us. Luckily, she agreed.

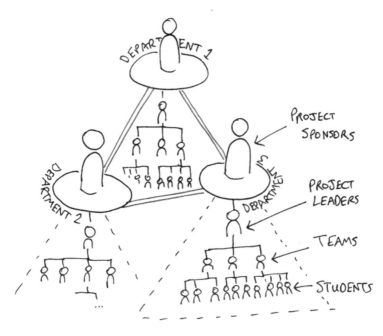

I sent the three leaders the usual preparation questions to let them know what I'd be looking and listening for during the meeting:

- When you're working at your best, you're like what?
- What is an ideal team that allows you to work at your best?
- Currently the Centre of Excellence in Teaching and Learning (CETL) project is like what?
- If this project were to be working perfectly it would be like what?

I wrote their answers on flip charts and put them up in the meeting room, to refer to when issues cropped up; I could use them to explore and resolve differences between the leaders. Some responses were metaphoric and some quite cognitive and I accepted them all equally. I planned to train their attention on their outcomes and to highlight any discrepancies between what they wanted to have happen and what they were doing in the moment.

I wanted to train their attention on what was actually happening between them but I also wanted these questions available to direct their attention towards their needs and outcomes. I still went in with a modelling mind, no desire to sell, just high quality attention on what was happening, what they wanted to have happen and what it might be useful to feed back to them in the moment.

I'll call the two colleagues from the other departments Mr M and Ms E. Through the meeting, I picked up on their conversational metaphors and noted their individual values for use later. Sarah's metaphors were all about efficiency, speed and positive relationships for students. Mr M's attention was on how the funding would help research goals they already had in place and Ms E's thinking was all about the transfer of knowledge and dissemination of research. I would use their outcomes as a reason for me intervening when their behaviour seemed at odds with what they stated they wanted to have happen. I would use the metaphors to ensure I was speaking their language and in rapport with their thinking.

For example, they all agreed that the project should be an example of excellence in teaching and learning, of getting the right balance between conveying information and fostering good learning relationships between people.

During the meeting Ms E brought out a massive document outlining the research requirements for the project. She was responsible for research and dissemination, which was a core part of the project.

She kept saying she was really worried that the rest of the project team weren't going to bother to read it. As she put the stack of papers on the table, I noticed a little bit of, "Yes, yes" impatience from Sarah and an almost imperceptible pushing back by Mr M, away from the table.

I was detecting drama in the system based on Ms E's agitation and the lack of mirroring or rapport between her and her two colleagues. What they were doing was not aligned to the outcomes they'd stated. It was neither an example of positive relationships nor of efficient transfer of knowledge and information. It didn't make obvious sense to me why there was drama so I thought it was worth unpacking. I wanted to name what I was noticing.

I thought, "I'll just go in on this one." I interrupted the flow and said something like:

Caitlin: **Can I just check, Ms E, you've done all of this work on research and evaluation and it's really, really important for the funders that this gets read and that all the different parts of the project are properly evaluated?**

Ms E: Yes, absolutely.

Caitlin: **And, can I just check ... Sarah, have you read it?**

Sarah: Well, no.

Caitlin: **And Mr M, have you read it?**

Mr M: No.

Caitlin: **What I'm noticing is that Ms E has said three times now that she's really concerned that people aren't going to take the evaluation seriously. You guys haven't read it and under her criteria you aren't taking it seriously and if you haven't, there's a good chance others haven't and neither is anyone else going to. Can I start with you, Sarah? What's happening that means you haven't read it?**

EVIDENCE

You guys haven't read it

INTERPRETATION

... under her criteria you aren't taking it seriously

IMPACT

...if you haven't, there's a good chance others haven't

CLEAN FEEDBACK

Sarah: Well, to be honest, it's huge, it's loads and loads of text and it looks impenetrable.

I wanted to stay with what was true for both Sarah and Ms E and make space for them to build a bridge towards a joint outcome. I was not in contempt, just unpacking what was happening for each of them.

I wanted to stay with what was true for both Sarah and Ms E and make space for them to build a bridge towards a joint outcome.

Caitlin: **So when** it's huge and looks impenetrable **AND** it's important for the funding of this project that everyone involved contributes to the evaluation, **what would you like to have happen?**

Sarah: I'd prefer a staff version that's lighter, simpler and for me and the other staff to use.

Ms E: OK, I can do that.

Caitlin: **Mr M, what's stopping you reading it?**

Mr M: There is so much research and evaluation going on in the department and to be honest, I know my boss doesn't really rate the research coming from Teaching and Learning so I just don't think it's that relevant to me.

Caitlin: **And when** you're a leader of CETL **AND** the project was awarded on the condition that you work as a team, sharing best practice, **and** you don't think your boss will value this research, **what would you like to have happen?**

Mr M: I need it shoved up my priorities. You'd need to get my boss to agree that research was a key part of this.

They were starting to get a feel for my interventions. I introduced the notion that it would be useful for them to understand one another's working patterns a bit better and we went into the preparation questions.

Caitlin: **When you are working at your best, you are like what?**

Sarah: I'm a fast car, impatient to get going, revving away and then speeding to the next destination.

Mr M: I'm a footballer, getting my ball in the top corner of the net. I need a very clear goal and a lot of confidence that I can do it.

Ms E: Well I have no idea what you're talking about, no idea at all. I can't get this metaphor stuff. I'm just organised, I'm really organised but they never give me what I need.

Caitlin: **And you can't get this metaphor stuff. And you're organised, really organised but they never give you what you need. And when they never give you what you need, that's like what?**

Suddenly, Ms E came out with this fantastic metaphor:

Ms E: Do you know what it's like? It's like I'm a 12-armed octopus trying to sort everything out and I'm in the sea and it's my job to grab every bit of detail about the

different projects from the very start and make them into a big piece
of evaluation. But people are already swimming off and starting their
projects without the big picture in mind. Sarah swims by occasionally,
and floats some stuff towards me, but not very much. And you, Mr
M, you are like a crab behind a rock – you're like a nasty little crab in
a dark hole and you never give me anything. And if I go in there to try
and get something, you pinch me.

The metaphor made all three of them laugh and there was shift in the quality of
the meeting. The other two recognised themselves and their attitude in Ms E's
metaphor landscape and they used it navigate around the problem and then to
facilitate one another to think about what they could do instead.

How often would Ms E like Sarah to swim by? Turns out much, much more
than Sarah would have imagined. Sarah made a note to make email contact
with Ms E at least weekly as they set up the project and to get all the Sport
Development people to copy Ms E into emails about ideas they were planning to
develop.

What could Mr M do to be less crabby? Facilitate a meeting between his boss
and Ms E, championing the requirement for collaboration if his department
wanted a full share of the funding.

To use a metaphor I first heard from Penny Tompkins, cleanly modelling a
group like this is like trying to untangle a knotted necklace chain. You don't want
to pull on any one strand in case you knot it tighter. You gently loosen a strand
here and a strand there until it begins to unravel itself.

Now Sarah was able to say, "OK, I see that if we hadn't sorted this out, the
project was possibly doomed to fail from an evaluation perspective. Ms E would
have badgered us and created more and more detail and evidence for what she
needed and why we had to do it. I'd have withdrawn more and Mr M and I
would have bitched about her. We wouldn't have been able to evidence any
collaborative research."

As the hour's meeting drew to a close I said, "This is the kind of thing I'll be
doing with the whole group. Will it be useful to you?" And there was a, "Yes,
absolutely, I can't wait to see you do this with The Boss", and so they brought me
in to design the awayday, send out the preparation work and facilitate the day.

Every meeting was like a voyage into the unknown, and there were and are risks
to this approach. If you count my first meeting with Sarah, plus the preparation

and now this group meeting, I'd already done more than a full day's work and I still hadn't been paid anything for my time or expertise. Also, I was only dealing with the project leaders; not the budget holding bosses above them. It might end up as nothing. On the other hand, I now had access to the whole of the system for a whole day and if I'd taken up Sarah's first invitation, it was obvious that a two-hour workshop wouldn't have had any real impact.

I had nothing to sell at this stage apart from my attention because I had no idea what we were going to do. I knew we'd probably use the Systemic Modelling™ tools including:

- Clean Questions
- Clean Set Up
- Clean Feedback
- Developmental Tasks
- Drama Triangle
- Clarifying Problems and moving to Outcomes
- Moving from Drama to Action using the Karma Cycle
- Eliciting metaphors such as Working at Best, Learning at Best, etc.

But I was unlikely to be able to sell these tools to them - they're almost meaningless without a clear context and an outcome.

The budget holders agreed that I could run the day and I restarted the Clean Scoping process again, this time with the three heads of department, followed by preparation questions across the whole team and bringing together their joint and disparate outcomes for the awayday.

The Structure of the Awayday

In the three departmental groups we did a Clean Set Up, the Five Senses exercise and some warm ups around when they were working at their best and an ideal team for them. I was facilitating Sarah's group with her boss and the rest of her team. I asked:

Caitlin:	**If this CETL project were to go just as you'd like, it will be like what?**
Sarah:	It'll be unclear.

The Boss: Oh that's typical of you to just be negative about everything! I'm not going to have your attitude ruining our project.

This seemed like high drama from nowhere and I was momentarily knocked sideways. It didn't make obvious sense so I figured it needed some careful unpacking. I didn't want to join in the drama in any way, either by rescuing Sarah or trying to deflect away from the tension. I wanted to unpack it and help the group to get to the structure of what was happening and to have some simple tools to handle this kind of conflict in the future. I rebalanced myself and stood up in the group. I stepped in between the two people and spoke to the group.

> I didn't want to join in the drama in any way, either by rescuing Sarah or trying to deflect away from the tension.

Caitlin: **I want to show you a really simple tool for turning this kind of interaction into useful information. First of all let's start with The Boss.** *(Turns attention to The Boss.)* **When something's** unclear, unclear **is like what?**

The Boss: It's like you've got your head up against a brick wall, you're in the dark. You can't see where you're going.

I wasn't looking at Sarah, the other person in the interaction. All of my attention in this moment was on The Boss. And I repeated for clarification:

Caitlin: You've got your head up against a brick wall, you're in the dark. You can't see where you're going.

The Boss: Yeah.

I turned back to the group and said, "Can you see that, for The Boss, Sarah wants the project to be like you've got your heads against brick walls, you're in the dark and can't see where you're going. Does it make sense why The Boss might have a strong reaction to this?" They nodded.

I was turning the contempt into information by helping the individuals and the group see how it made sense, from a certain perspective. To do this, I had to have really strong compassion for both Sarah and for The Boss, simultaneously. I turned to Sarah:

> I was turning the contempt into information by helping the individuals and the group see how it made sense, from a certain perspective.

Caitlin: **And when the project's unclear, unclear is like what?"**

Sarah: It's like so far we've had to go along railway tracks or follow a road that's already laid out for us. But for this project to be really good for me, we've got just the landscape opening out in front of us with no defined way ahead.

Caitlin: **And when there's** no defined way ahead, **what happens next?**

Sarah: We are free to think what's the best way for us to navigate through this landscape, we can actually think new thoughts and not have to follow the track that's already been laid.

I turned to the group again…

Caitlin: **So when The Boss hears** unclear **it means** brick wall and in the dark **and when Sarah uses** unclear **it means** a landscape opening out, and thinking what's the best way to navigate through it. **Are you noticing that difference?**

They nodded.

Caitlin: **Did you hear what I said to get this information? It's very simple. Write it down.**

I got the group to write down:

- When you hear X, X is like what?
- And when you say X, X is like what?
- When X is like Y for you and X is like Z for you, what would you like to have happen now?

The Boss said, "Yeah, but what Sarah's just said is not unclear, that's uncharted." Viewing this from a drama perspective, The Boss was still taking a persecuting position, that her interpretation of 'unclear' was OK and Sarah's was not OK. I didn't want to introduce the Drama Triangle at this stage but I would remember this as an illustration for later on. I felt the group had learned enough and that it was time to move on. I turned back to the whole group again:

Caitlin: **OK, so can you hear that while The Boss knows what Sarah means by** unclear**, the word** unclear **had such a strong meaning for her that it still means** banging her head against a brick wall? **Sarah, would it be OK to call the** opening landscape and the new thoughts and the navigating 'uncharted'**?**
Sarah: **Yeah, that's alright.**
Caitlin: **So you'd like** the project to be a landscape opening up **and for** you all to think 'What's the best way for us to navigate through this landscape?' **Who's got a different metaphor for how you'd like this project to be?"**

When someone is cross, bored or withdrawing from the group, I take what is happening in the moment and explore it. The chances are that whatever is going on, it's important enough for them to move to action. Rather than getting contemptuous about conflict, or thinking, "This is getting a bit out of hand... I'd better step in here," I relax and get curious about what I'll find when it gets unpacked. I assume that I – and the group and the individuals – can handle whatever's happening.

I keep in mind, "What's the least I have to do here?" My job is to inspire them to feel more capable to manage themselves and one another in the future.

> I keep in mind, "What's the least I have to do here?" My job is to inspire them to feel more capable to manage themselves and one another in the future.

If I can help them find out what kinds of things are important enough to produce action in this group then they can share their highest values. Once the group are clearer about their values they can use these to motivate themselves to get things done.

There are a number of ways that Systemic Modelling™ helps people get to know what's important to them, including the preparation questions, Clean Set Up and the Five Senses exercise. All of these are priming the individual systems and the group as a whole so that the facilitator can bring conflict into the here and now and then to unpack it in a fun, non-judgemental way.

This unpacking is what inspires them to catch themselves and one another in-the-moment and to have the skills and confidence to unpack whatever is actually going on. This allows the group to live more in the present and to make richer connections and better use of the expertise and experience of everyone in the room.

It can be exhilarating for a group who may have felt crippled by these conflictual exchanges in the past.

After a successful awayday, the three CETL leaders had a much clearer goal for what they wanted to achieve overall. The Boss was keen that they keep me and Systemic Modelling™ around and the team wanted to learn how to do what they'd seen me do.

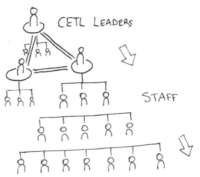

We decided that I would just work in the one department as the other two bosses weren't as interested in learning how to create self-modelling groups and for this project I wanted a really tight sphere of influence in which I had strong champions.

The university project emerged in layers over the next two years. I'll just include some of the pivotal points in this case study that show Systemic Modelling™ in action and how different groups began to inspire capability in one another.

Creating a Peer Coaching Network

Sarah had already bought in to the idea that change had to start from the top, so the most experienced and successful lecturers within the department were invited to join together as a peer coaching network. They'd be modelling good practice already in the system, and it would be a small pilot so that the project was being led by example.

We began with one-to-one interviews for 'When you're teaching at your best, you're like what?' During these individual clean coaching sessions they developed embodied metaphors for being at their best and then expanded the metaphors using Robert Dilts's logical levels by thinking about the environments, behaviours, skills, beliefs, values and identity that supported them to teach at their best. They took their initial models, reflected on them, refined them and came back for a second session to consider what they could do to teach at their best even more of the time. They identified particular strengths and also areas they wanted to develop. Each individual created a 'Rough Guide to Me at My Best' including:

- A metaphor for 'me teaching at my best'.
- What you'll see and hear when I'm at my best.
- Expanded detail about what supports or stops me being at my best.
- Areas I'd like to develop and that are open to observation and peer coaching.
- Three things colleagues can do to support me.

These 'Rough Guides' were shared across the staff team and set the tone for the rest of the project.

The Sports Successes DVD:
Paying Due Diligence before Moving to Action

One of the projects that had already started was the filming for an inspirational DVD for the students, with some very successful people from the sports industry.

Sarah invited me to be the interviewer of the 'successes' and I sat in on a development meeting with the staff team as they discussed who they knew and who they could persuade to be a part of the project. One knew the gymnast Beth Tweddle, while another was bringing Kate Walsh, captain of the British Hockey team.

As I sat in on the meeting I observed that all of the attention of the meeting was on bringing the best people to the project but not on the purpose of the making the DVD. I couldn't tell how they had decided that it would be a good idea to make this DVD. Even though it wasn't really my meeting, I hesitantly asked.

Caitlin: **Can I just check, what's the purpose of the DVD?**

Sarah: To inspire students to make the most of their time at university so that they get as much as possible from it.

The meeting continued.

Caitlin: **Can I just check … You're all lecturers in Sport here, did you** make the most of your time at university?

I was looking for examples of where the outcome has already been achieved from within the current system. Most of them nodded.

Caitlin: **So … What** inspired **you** to get the most from it?

Donna: Oh for me it was my grandfather. He was a dock worker and a great reader. He drummed it into all of us that getting an education made us free and that it was a great privilege. I was determined to make him proud of me.

Caitlin: **Who's different to that?**

Ivan: For me it was financial. I decided to take a break in my career as a personal trainer to get a degree. It put my wife and kids in a difficult position so I had to work really hard to justify taking the time out of work.

Caitlin: **So,** financial **and** justifying your time out of work, making your granddad proud ... **Who's different again?**

Every person in the room had a different story and not one of those stories involved being inspired by elite athletes or successes in their field of study.

Caitlin: **So each of you achieved the outcomes that you want for those students and yet not one of you was inspired by an elite athlete. So what kind of DVD is needed?**

There was a lively discussion and they decided that they wanted the DVD to support the students to get the most out of their time at university, regardless of their abilities. I suggested that we find a group of students and adults some of whom had and some of whom hadn't got the most of their time at university and modelled them.

We had a clean research project! We interviewed around 30 final year students and lecturers one-to-one and in focus groups, asking, "What is the difference that made the difference to you getting the most from your time at university?" I expanded their answers using clean questions and regularly asking "Who's not like that?" in the focus groups to encourage diverse views. I taped the interviews and transcribed them and analysed them for repeating themes. Five key themes emerged from the data:

- Understanding how you learn.
- Being able to use time effectively.
- Making good decisions.
- Getting over things when they go wrong and learning from the mistake.
- Staying motivated and inspired.

I suggested that if they wanted the students, as a body, to get more from their time at university, then it would be a good idea if the students paid attention and developed their self-awareness in these five areas. If they did this in groups then they could also learn strategies from one another for keeping themselves learning and working at their best. They would all have developed three embodied metaphors models for learning, time and decision making and then two more conversational models for mistakes and inspiration.

With the athletes and the studio already booked I suggested that instead of interviewing the successes, I could cleanly model them and find out how each of them responded to these themes. This way the students could compare their own models with those of the people on the DVD, giving them an extra description. This became the Learning Journeys DVD and has been a great resource for students in the university and for Clean Language learners around the world. It is a way of having an insight into very different ways of experiencing the world, even if you haven't got your own group to practice with.

Serendipity: Six Metaphors for Emergent Knowledge

At this point there was another serendipitous shift in the development of Systemic Modelling™. I'd noticed that most of our business work followed the Metaphors at Work process that I'd first designed for the software company. We went into teams and elicited three metaphors, sometimes four: working at best; ideal team; current organisation; desired organisation. This seemed adequate for getting the team to be able to understand where each member was coming from and then be able to predict how each of them might approach a given task. The group developed deeper collective trust and worked more effectively as a team. But I also had a feeling that something quite different had happened with the young people at the youth project, with the software company and with the long-term unemployed. As well as developing trust, they'd seemed to make big shifts in their behaviours towards one another and their attitudes towards what was possible, for themselves and for one another. They seemed, as individuals and as a group, transformed by the process and were able to use the tools to carry on transforming when new issues arose. They didn't just understand their patterns, they no longer seemed so constrained by them. What I didn't know yet was what might be making that difference.

I was lucky enough to be spending time with David Grove again. He'd been away trialling, developing and teaching his latest processes – Clean Space, Emergent Knowledge and the Power of Six – and was now working closely with my husband, psychotherapist Shaun Hotchkiss, using our house as one of his UK bases. David's Clean Space process was really exciting. He was encouraging his clients to find six different positions or spaces from which to engage with a symptom. He'd ask them two or three questions in each of the six spaces and then move on. The first, second and third spaces were all about understanding what was happening and coming to know the symptom better. However, when his clients were invited to move to the fourth, fifth and sixth spaces, their understanding transformed and they

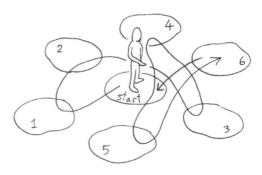

were no longer bound by the issues, beliefs or trauma that had been present at position one. There was something about moving through the six positions that gave them freedom from their symptom.

I discussed with David the correlations between his new ideas and my group process. Was there a similar shift happening at a group level? Three metaphors for predictability and six for freedom from old behaviours? I reflected on the different projects and could see with the youth project that while all of the metaphors had engaged the young people, it was when they shared the fifth and sixth metaphors that they'd started advocating for one another and modelling new behaviours that weren't instigated by me. At the software company they'd really enjoyed and benefited from the four models they'd built and shared during the Metaphors at Work process, but it was during the extra metaphor elicitations in the last three days that they started transforming the way that they worked together. I decided to aim towards six metaphors in each culture change project.

Staff Team - Leading by Example

To this end, once a week, at the start of a staff meeting, the team chose a theme from our research project and began modelling themselves and one another:

- When you're learning at your best, you're like what?
- Time is like what?
- When you're making good decisions, that's like what?
- What are some examples when something's gone wrong and you've got over it? What factors supported you to get over it?
- What inspires and motivates you?

Just as Sarah had hoped, they came to understand one another's values and intentions much better. Being educators, even those who loved the modelling and meta-learning, they challenged why they needed to get to know one another like this and how it would help their students learn. One senior lecturer said, "I don't get how understanding one another's metaphors makes a difference to teaching. I mean if I know your metaphors how does that benefit me or you for that matter?"

I remembered that when this lecturer was sharing his model for teaching at his best he called himself Spider Dan, in the centre of a web of attention. He valued making lots of connections and linking lots of different academic areas at once. He also kept his lectures personally relevant as well as academically interesting by remembering information about each student. With his metaphor in mind, I went to the white board and drew a dot in the centre and said,

Caitlin: Well if you think about it there are two main reasons for students to develop awareness of their own metaphors and of one another's. Once a student knows his or her metaphors for learning, organising time, decision making etc. *(I drew five dots around the central dot)*... then they are able to make connections between how they organize time and how they learn at their best, they understand how to use motivation to keep them to their deadlines. They can use this information to keep themselves learning well.

I drew lines between the dots and the student in the centre.

Caitlin: Then as they build up alternative models of how their fellow students think and act and do the same with their lecturers…

I drew a second layer of dots around the first and started making lines between them.

Caitlin: ...they can see where there are connections and where there are disconnects and then they build up a sense of who'll be easiest or most difficult to learn from and make adjustments accordingly.

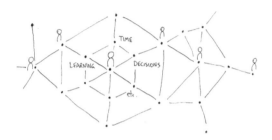

As the 'web' built up Danny started nodding enthusiastically.

Danny: Yes, that's what our students need to do, build up a network of responses - I get it now. That's brilliant."

Caitlin: **So Danny, how is it that the project makes more sense to you when I explain it like this?**

Danny: It just feels right ... I'm not sure ... It's all about the students making multiple connections and keeping track of what's going on... Oh, you've done it as a web ... OK, I get it.

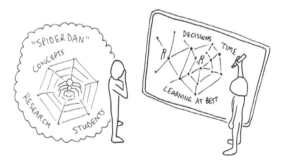

It's important that these kinds of interactions are not about showing off, although I confess I do enjoy the showmanship, but that they are about having a relationship with each person's stuff that then allows you to behave in a way that really speaks to how they organise information. What could be more respectful than that?

Metaphors at Work with the Staff Team

The staff explored all five themes that had emerged from the research, developing self-knowledge of what they were asking their students to do. I then ran the Metaphors at Work process with ten members of the staff team, which meant they developed nine different models for the way they thought about things.

As the staff developed a joint metaphor for their department, I noticed a big shift in their relationships, energy and enthusiasm. They excitedly started to throw ideas around and ask one another clarification questions and then suddenly came up with the idea of a well-laid-out retail store, similar to Ikea.

In their metaphor you arrive at the store and there are beautiful rooms all designed to give you an idea of how things could look. All the work has been done for you and the rooms are there to pique your interest and to show you how things can fit together. In the next floor there's more freedom to move between the bathroom area, lighting, bedrooms etc. You can see where the things on the first floor came from. On the third floor you gather together the components that you've decided you want and you create something original and unique to you. Then you take your purchases out of the shop and off into the outside world.

They mapped out the tightly guided spoon-fed study of the first year, the learning-to-learn of the second year and finally the self-guided research of the final year. They got so excited about their retail store and how much it helped them communicate about different modules and how they all fit together that they commissioned design students from a different area of the university to build it as a 3-D model that they could use in a hands-on session with students. They used this model to demonstrate to students how different lectures fit together and all of the different paths they could take to complete their study. Now the staff were operating more as a learning community, all ready to design the student programme from a position of using the process themselves.

They were delighted with their 'learning object', as they liked to call their team model. I started to consider how to create learning objects of my own. How could I translate the Systemic Modelling™ tools and processes into products that would be available for the staff and students to play with after I'd left? I was focussed on the transferability of the model at this stage. I wanted the student body to have the same high degree of modelling skills as we'd seen in the super coaches at the whole school but without me having to train them directly. They had the Learning Journeys DVD, what else could we make?

The Student Tutorial Programme

Together with the staff team we designed a self-modelling programme for the students based around the five key themes. We created, with the help of the talented Marian Way, three years' worth of self-modelling workbooks. As well as the key themes, we included the Karma Cycle and asked the students to set weekly and monthly outcomes based on things they'd learned. As well as self-modelling with metaphors we also introduced the Triune Brain, the Drama Triangle and an adaptation of the Problem, Remedy, Outcome (PRO) model developed by Penny and James, so that students and staff could recognise when they were problem and when they were outcome focussed and could choose where to put their attention.

The first book focussed on self-awareness, the second on developing awareness of others and peer coaching skills and the final book focussed on students putting this learning into practice to sustain themselves and their peers through their dissertation. The books alternated between clean modelling and developing personal metaphors and then putting that learning into action to improve their experience at university. The university staff each had a group of ten students and they met as a tutorial group and kept the same group over the three years. The books were designed as diaries that the students needed to use for other reasons besides modelling such as putting in their deadlines for assignments and specific goals assigned by lecturers. This kept the models in their minds outside of tutorials and the students were regularly seen getting their books out in lessons to keep notes in.

To demonstrate how the modelling worked with students I'll introduce Matt. Matt was a nightmare for his tutor. He seemed inattentive in lectures, never gave his work in on time to get provisional feedback, was often late, fell asleep in lectures and in tutorials and then suddenly, without warning, would pull an all-nighter and write and deliver a perfectly good piece of work at the very last minute. It was frustrating because they could see that he was capable of achieving much better marks but his lack of planning meant he wasn't getting the support he needed to update his work.

When Matt developed his metaphor for learning at his best he was a cheetah:

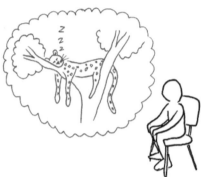

- I lie around all day in a tree, sleeping, then something catches my eye or I get hungry, I'm really fast, kill it, eat it and then I'm back in my tree again.

He compared his metaphor with those of his peers and was amused by the differences. They set themselves Developmental Tasks to explore and improve their learning but he didn't bother.

The next month when they explored their models for time, the other students described time as a line or a circle or a path and described how events and processes were often laid out so that they knew what was coming up. They discussed how they could use their metaphor models to set goals that were compelling for them. Matt said:

- I don't really know what you're talking about. I don't have a time line. Time's more like a big cloud. I'm just in it and it's hazy, then an opportunity or a deadline looms into view and consumes my attention and then it's all cloudy again.

For their third metaphor, decision making, Matt listened to his colleagues again and said:

- I don't really make decisions, it's more that I'm just following the flow, cruising along and then something jolts me along a new path ... hang on, this is the same pattern. I'm not in control of anything. I'm always

reacting to what I have to do
or what comes into my way.

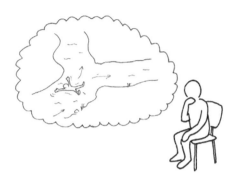

After three metaphors, Matt
was no longer just having his
metaphors run his life without his
awareness. He started to see his
patterns repeated everywhere and
began to wonder where they came
from and what other options he
had.

By the time his group were modelling their fourth and fifth metaphors, Matt
was detecting the pattern of his patterns, comparing them to some of the nine
alternative models available from his peer group and another seven models from
the Learning Journey DVD.

Matt then used the Karma Cycle to interrupt his patterns and to try out new
behaviours and get feedback. For example:

Clean Set Up

- If this week were to go just as I'd like, it will be like being at a busy theme
  park with friends. There'll be times when I just follow the crowd and be
  on whatever ride they gravitate towards. And there'll be times when I'm
  deliberately choosing which part of the park to go to next and making
  sure I get there.
- For it to be like that I need to be tall and decisive and use all of my senses
  to decide where to take myself next.
- I'll need to set a timer on my phone, once a day, to spend five minutes
  making my own decisions about how I'll use time that day. Like a wake-
  up call to put my head above the crowd and decide where to go next in
  my theme park.

Developmental Task

- Tomorrow I'll set my phone alarm for 8.30am and I'll get a big sheet of
  paper out and draw three activities for the day and put them in order.
  I'll programme my phone to set an alarm when it's time to start a new
  thing.

- If I'm not doing it I'll be somewhere I hadn't planned or just ignoring my phone alarm.
- When I am doing it I'll be putting my paper up on the kitchen wall and moving from one activity to the next, really enjoying the activity once I get there and then being reminded to move to the next.

Matt was able to make a more conscious decision about when to go with the flow and when to set himself a goal and achieve it. He asked his tutorial group to help him keep on the path until he'd achieved his commitments.

In the first year we didn't expect the students to necessarily understand why they were being asked to develop the metaphors. We just made them an activity that everyone did. Some students got it straight away, some did it because they were being asked to and it was engaging enough to keep their interest. However by the third year the students regularly reported that the tutorial course had made the biggest difference to them being able to successfully navigate through their time at university, to make successful decisions and to keep themselves and their colleagues motivated throughout.

They understood and used one another's metaphors and coached one another from problems through to outcomes and actions.

There were two out of the ten staff members who weren't fully engaged with the modelling process and who didn't support the clean modelling in the tutorials but their students still had their workbooks and the learning DVD's and we hoped that, like in the school, these students would become part of the new culture simply because this kind of thinking was part of the student experience.

This project had followed the full Systemic Modelling™ process now; from Clean Scoping to Metaphors at Work to bringing the skills to students and applying the Karma Cycle to creating a learning to learn culture across the department. The process was working well in tutorials and across the staff team but it wasn't yet spreading further than the project I'd designed with them.

The last part of the project was where the staff began asking themselves, "What would we need to be doing now so that the behaviours we want from our students just fall out as a natural consequence of the way we do things around here."

Using Clean Feedback in Essay Marking

One day while in Sarah's office I noticed written feedback she'd given a student. One comment said, "Great point, well done." And another said, "Needs work." I looked at the comments and thought, "I have no idea what 'great point' she's talking about or what section 'needs work' or what kind of work.

I knew that Sarah liked one point and that something needed work but I had no idea what I'd do with that information if I was going to re-write the essay. I went to Sarah saying, "I'm noticing this feedback isn't as specific or usable as the Clean Feedback model the students use in their tutorials." And she said, "Oh yes, but when you've got a hundred student essays to mark you don't have time to put that level of detail in."

I could feel the incongruence between putting in a small amount of work that wasn't useful, more a tick-box action, and Sarah's high value of looking after the student well-being and ensuring they had a great learning experience. I could feel some modelling coming on.

Caitlin: **When a student reads their feedback, what would you like to have happen?**

Sarah: I want them to take it on board and put it into practice in their next essay or re-write this one.

Caitlin: **And what would this student, with this essay, put into practice?**

Sarah: *(Picks up essay and scans it.)* Well to be honest, I don't really know what I meant by these comments; I'd have to re-read the essay.

If Sarah couldn't make sense of her own feedback without re-reading the whole essay, the student probably wouldn't be able to either. If Sarah had marked over 100 essays at this level of non-specificity then that was over 100 small amounts of effort that would have no impact on student performances. Across a staff team that is so many hours of wasted effort. Surely they should either give no feedback or ensure their feedback was of high enough quality to be acted upon?

Caitlin: **And** you'd have to re-read the essay **to make sense of it. And what do students want to have happen with their essay feedback?**

Sarah: Oh, students always report that the feedback isn't of high enough quality and it isn't timely enough for them to do anything with it. I guess by the time they get it, like me, they'd have to re-read the whole essay to try to work out what I meant. They probably think it's a waste of their time.

Caitlin: **When** students would have to re-read their whole essay **and** they probably think that feedback is a waste of time, **what would you like to have happen now?**

Sarah: Well, I'd really like students to be able to read their feedback and act on it, do something with it.

Caitlin: **And what would need to happen for that to happen?**

The next few minutes were a struggle with me picking up both sides of the argument and Sarah flipping between her reality and what she wished was true.

Sarah: Well I can't ask staff to give higher quality feedback; no one will do that voluntarily and I can't make the staff do that... But if we don't improve our feedback the whole thing is worth nothing and we may as well give no feedback. We know it isn't working as it is… But there'll be a riot from staff, they say the students don't ever read it anyway so what's the point? But then if you think about it, why would they read it. I can't even understand my own feedback to them.

I stuck with it, holding her to her outcomes, bringing the outcomes and the problems into the same space, summarising and asking what she wanted to have happen...

Caitlin: **So when** there'll be a riot**, and** you want students to put feedback into practice **and** there isn't enough time to give better feedback, **and** the students complain that feedback isn't timely enough … **What would you like to have happen now?**

… until she spontaneously came up with an idea that she thought would work: Rather than agonise over it herself, she'd bring this complex problem to the staff team, put it in the centre of the group, highlight both sides of the problem and ask the team what they'd like to have happen. This way she'd be able to use all of their different experiences and expertise and they'd come up with a solution together that they would all be able to sign up to.

At the staff meeting Sarah facilitated it beautifully:

Sarah: Here's what the students are reporting about feedback … Here's what the staff say about feedback … Here's how we want our students to improve … We've got the Clean Feedback model that the students use to give to one another. What would we like to have happen with feedback?

The staff then started thinking about the issue, not in terms of a single essay, but the feedback a student got over a year.

They designed a simple student feedback sheet with sections for *evidence*, *inference* and *impact*. They'd use this sheet to log what they'd just read that got their attention and then what they inferred about it and the impact it had on the mark the student received.

Example of Clean Feedback in essays:

Evidence: In five paragraphs, there's only one reference.
Inference: You haven't done enough background reading.
Impact: I've dropped your mark down from 58 to a 50.

What to do next time:

Evidence: I want to see one reference for every point you make; two to three references per 100 words ideally from three difference sources
Inference: You'd researched the topic and were thinking deeply about your argument.
Impact: This change alone would take this essay mark up over a 60.

The staff found it easy to use the sheet while marking and also easy to test whether the students had put the feedback into action. The students found it easy to implement and each effort made by staff could translate into a positive impact on student attainment.

Student Induction - Just the Way We Do Things Around Here

From this point onwards, the staff started to do more things independently of me and having decided that they wanted their students to get this thinking from the very start, they overhauled their induction process. They decided to make the first five weeks all about developing self-awareness and about students building the relationships and networks that would support them over the three years.

Instead of a one-week induction consisting of fresher's week with copious amounts of alcohol and then straight into lectures, they decided to make induction a five-week process that introduced students to themselves, their learning styles, their lecturers and their teaching styles.

This induction process is still happening. Each week, they take one of the five themes starting with, "When you're learning at your best, you're like what?" The students have a first pass at considering their learning style and at the same time all across that week are mini-introductions to courses, lectures, sport, games, group work etc. The students are encouraged to form and reform into collaborative groups allowing them to forge a number of relationships across the department, rather than just the people in the lectures they choose. They meet all of the staff team and are encouraged to see the connections between the different courses in a way that was unthinkable before we started the project. During the second week they examine 'time' in a similar way, then on week three, 'decision-making', until all the themes have been explored.

This was a revolutionary way to start a university course but of course for the students arriving, it was 'just the way we do things around here'; they rarely had any experience of other ways of doing things.

In terms of creating an iterative learning process, it was poetry for me and it was a microcosm of the year ahead of them – so that when they started their lectures, were introduced to their self-modelling workbooks and were asked again, "When you're learning at your best, you're like what?" the question wasn't new or strange and they could get more from it. They had so many opportunities to form groups to achieve an outcome that sharing their ideas in a tutorial group, for the purpose of learning about themselves and learning from others, was already a familiar concept.

Coordinating Personal & Academic Learning

Another move that seemed like genius to me was when Sarah asked the staff team to coordinate their lectures with the topics being discussed in the tutorial groups. This meant that when the students were exploring, for example, their personal models for time and setting themselves Developmental Tasks to use time more effectively, then within each lecture in the following month there would be reference to time. What's the relationship between time and elite athleticism? What are the hours it takes for mastery of a sport? What's the relationship between time, leisure and diversity? Does the time when a sport is offered affect who in the community is able to access it?

This way the students were able to train their attention internally to their own model, externally to other people's models and then into their subject matter and of course to write up their understanding in the essays after each lecture, adding weight and value to the tutorial discussions.

The staff were now doing things that were not predictable from the tools I gave them. They'd internalised the methodology and were using it to create new processes. They were the modellers now.

Trainee Teachers Take It Into Schools

It wasn't just the staff who were creating new applications. A group of trainee teachers were talking about how their school placements had gone and one reported that she was teaching some pupils to vault and when one of them went over the vaulting horse, she said:

Teacher: **What do you think about that?**
Pupil: Oh it was boss miss.
Teacher: **So, what did you see or hear when you call it** boss?
Pupil: Well when she went over the horse, she landed on both feet and she didn't wobble, and then she stood straight, stopped a minute and looked ahead.
Teacher: **And when you see that, what does it mean for you?**
Pupil: It looked like she was really, really in control.

She told me, "The more I do Clean Feedback with them the more articulate they're getting."

This department was capable of producing teachers more able to help young people learn to distinguish between what was presented to them and what they were inferring. This was the kind of thing I'd been hoping for from the early youth project and I felt excited wondering what else these young teachers would do with the tools for pupils in the future.

Longer Term Results

It is not possible to make any causal relationships between the development of this project and student attainment. We didn't have a control group and the project outcomes were emerging as we went along. We didn't have a true baseline with which to compare our results.

However, in the five years before the start of this project, the average number of students in this department attaining a first or upper second-class degree was 49%. In the three years following the staff development process and the start of the student self-modelling programme, student attainment rose year on year to 56% then 63% then 73%. Up until the publication of this book the attainment figure has remained between 73% and 75% and the retention on this course has been at 97%.

Sarah was delighted with the changes she'd noticed in staff and in student behaviour. Staff reported that students were less likely to depend on their tutors for help, relying more on strong networks between peers. They developed strategies for being able to learn from lecturers whose teaching style didn't match their learning style and by the second and third years were able to articulate how they were doing this. They'd become more reflective in their behaviour and by the third year were becoming reflexive – taking their learning and feeding forward to ensure they get the most out of forthcoming situations.

The students carried their self-modelling books from lecture to lecture and used the DVD to bolster their learning. There is even a mural in the entrance to the department created by Sarah and a group of her students on learning metaphors with clean questions on the walls.

Last year, Sarah's tutor group of nine students all achieved First Class honours degrees. This is unheard of in a mixed ability tutorial group and I asked her what was the difference that made the difference. She said, "It's the first time I've seen

my tutor group operate as a fully independent learning community. I just kept coming in and saying, "Well done!" or, "I believe in you" and "If you really want a First I'm sure you can do it." They got each other's patterns early on in the first year and then they coached, badgered, supported and nurtured each other through the second and third years. In the end the two weakest of the students couldn't bear to be left behind and the stronger students wouldn't let them. They were all so delighted when the whole group got Firsts."

Cautionary Tale

This case study is a great example of Systemic Modelling™ in action. It was relatively inexpensive to set up and has had lasting results. It was working well for those students whose tutors loved the process as well as for those who paid it lip-service. It was across the department. My caution is around the hope and expectations that can follow great results.

I had expected other departments within the wider university, or at the very least within the same faculty, to be clamouring for the process and keen to have the same improved relationships, results and retention for their own students.

Instead, the initial response from the surrounding departments was straight off the Drama Triangle. Some took victim positions, claiming that they couldn't get their staff on board or that it couldn't possibly work with their students. Some took a rescuer role as though we were saying their students weren't good enough. They stated that their students were perfectly capable of managing themselves and didn't need any kind of babying or monthly tutorials. Perhaps saddest of all were the persecutor positions where colleagues outside of the department talked of this team as being too full of themselves and even claiming they were forming a learning cult.

But, over the following years, as the results have maintained and the ideas aren't quite so new to the rest of the university, some aspects of the project such as the five-week induction and the Clean Feedback forms for students are now being adopted by other departments. The metaphor question, "When you're teaching at your best, you're like what?" and the outcome question, "What would you like to have happen?" also pop up in odd places around the university.

The use of metaphors for collaboration is also finding a footing. One head of a different faculty, who had been part of the original awayday, came up to me a year or so after the project was complete and said, "We were having a big departmental meeting the other day and it was going really badly when someone said, "Let's stop and think about what each of us actually wants here. If this department were just as we'd like, it would be like what?" We had some ideas and then we came up with the metaphor of creating a new garden that we all loved being in. We worked out who would be doing the preparation, the sowing and the reaping of the fruit and how far in the future we were planting the garden for. Then we were off and the whole thing sorted itself out."

So there's hope that as long as people are finding bits and pieces useful the reach will spread over time.

Last Word from Sarah

"The project has completely changed the way I think, the way all of us think. I don't do all of it. For example I don't run a Clean Set Up in a staff meeting but I always do it with my students at the start of the term and I do it myself before a difficult meeting or a piece of work. It hasn't always been easy and maybe if I'd known how far the journey would be, I'd never have started. But it's revolutionised the way we do things, the way we talk to each other and also what we aspire to get from our students. It's not that we don't go into drama, or play victim, or bitch about people. We do still do that, but we also think differently and challenge each other. Instead of keeping the drama going, we start thinking about what we would like to have happen instead and what we could put in place to get it."

CHAPTER 8

Taking Stock

*Consolidating what we've got
and working out what's missing*

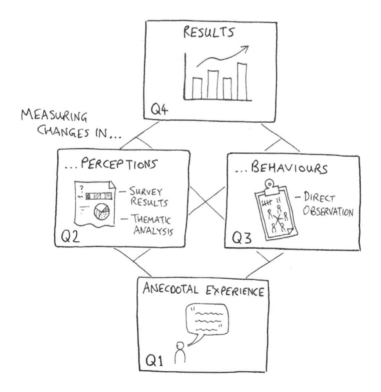

Around this time I began writing up the individual models, consolidating the approach, reflecting on the principles and noticing how the whole thing fitted together. It was 10 years since I'd set out on my compelling path and I felt I finally had a model worth sharing – an approach which:

- Allowed groups to become more present to what they cared about and more open to inquiring into one another's experience.
- Gave people the chance to name conflict and navigate gently into and through it to uncover its treasures.
- Encouraged teams to take the time and space to share individual outcomes and resolve the differences between them before embarking on a new course of action.

The original vision I'd had for how groups could take clean questions and use them together was becoming a reality. Along the way I'd also added in a number of other models that helped with shifting attention from modelling individual systems to modelling systems of individuals.

Clean questions, when used between a therapist and a client, support the therapist to be present to their client's words and gestures, to repeat them back and then direct attention to an aspect of their metaphor landscape. This creates space for new information and knowledge to emerge that is adjacent to what has already been said.

With Systemic Modelling™, we were applying similar principles across a group. As well as space being created *within* individual systems, this was also happening *between* the different individuals in the room. Group members were taking a contribution, asking one or two questions to be present to it and then asking, "Who's not like that?" or "Who has something different?" This created the opportunity to learn from one another as well as to share our own expertise.

All the models were aimed at creating balance between exploring what was happening and wondering what people would like to have happen. It was all about creating an agile group attention that was curious, compassionate and confident that resolution could be found.

Within the Karma Cycle, Clean Feedback supported the separation of what was being presented from what was being inferred and helped the giver and the receiver acknowledge difference without drama. Clean Set Up helped prepare individuals and groups to pay due diligence to their outcomes, their roles in achieving them and the resources they needed to get what they wanted. Developmental Tasks encouraged experimentation, trial and error and the courage to have a go and see what happened. This was how new behaviours were born and how new evidence emerged that it didn't have to be the way it had always been.

The Triune Brain model allowed people to recognise what kind of issue was going on. They could tell when they had gone 'reptilian' and were just tired or hungry or cold and getting into contempt because their basic needs weren't being met. They knew not to try to teach or learn when they were in their reptilian brains because that isn't a great place for accessing a good learning state. They could tell when the whole team was in their mammalian or reptilian brain. This might happen after a death in a family or when there is a new boss in the workplace and people couldn't make sense of things using the old rules. These models helped people make sense of a situation without going into drama about it.

The Drama Triangle helped people to identify when they were in contempt and to give a name to it. They could simply notice the drama, consider whether they'd gone into victim, persecutor or rescuer and also notice whether other people were on points of the triangle too. This model was useful for naming contempt and acknowledging that it happens. Then the groups could stop in the moment and explore what was happening, clarify it, resolve it and move on.

During the university project, a phrase kept coming up for me: *The patterns are starting to coalesce.* The tools and principles were fitting together to become a cohesive approach to culture change. At the same time as this coalescence, the tools were taking on a life of their own and they were being used in a pick-and-mix way .

A team might not be ready for the whole Metaphors at Work process but could easily take on some Clean Feedback to improve their appraisal system. We could introduce Clean Set Up as a tool for setting up more effective meetings without having to introduce any clean questions or metaphors. The Triune Brain was being taught to students so that they could use it to promote well-being during intense pressure to complete assignments or pass exams. The Drama Triangle was being used in families to interrupt the same old flare-ups and encourage people to consider what they actually wanted to have happen.

The facilitators who worked within Training Attention were also taking the tools from the tool kit and shaping them for specific needs:

- Cheryl Winter, who assisted throughout the university project, used Clean Set Up and Clean Feedback with her retail client to change the way managers dealt with internal complaints and to help staff to be more self-reliant.
- The author Richard W. Hardwick took the Five Senses exercise, along with clean questions, into his creative writing work in prisons. There, he supported women, men and young offenders, with sentences ranging from two months to natural life, to turn their internal experiences into pieces of poetry, autobiography, fiction and animation.
- Nancy Doyle and Emma Dalrymple adapted the Welfare to Work course, making it much more job-focussed, taking out the formal clean questions and honing it down to a six-day course to be run over three weeks. With their expertise and this new course structure, they increased the retention of clients on the course and got the job outcome rate up to 69% for the hardest to help unemployed.
- Patrick and I used Five Senses plus clean questions when we trained police officers to interview vulnerable witnesses without influencing their evidence.

As well as these targeted approaches we now had workbooks and manuals that we could leave with clients. With the help of Chris Grimsley and Glenda Sutcliffe, we'd created a training DVD about Clean Language and Systemic Modelling™ so that a wider audience had access to the tools and exercises. We could produce 'leave behind' training packages containing the tools and artefacts our clients would need to create their own internal staff trainings.

Despite all of these successes, some things were still not working well:

- I didn't have a clear description of the whole process that could be packaged in an attractive accessible way. Systemic Modelling™ still seemed too complex to explain during a single meeting.
- The pitch process was drawn out into a number of short interactions and small projects. I couldn't sell the process until they'd had personal experience and found a business value.
- We struggled to help clients to spread the idea of the processes wider than our project and this limited the sphere of influence we had. When their colleagues asked what they were doing differently they'd describe all sorts of things but find it difficult to put in a nutshell.

As my understanding of the models consolidated, something kept flickering in my peripheral vision. I felt sure that a bit was missing, something that would help to hang the whole thing together. This flickering happened when people asked me what the benefit would be of running a Systemic Modelling™ project. I'd start telling them how their people would be paying attention to themselves and one another with curiosity rather than contempt and how the group would communicate with less drama and more action. Instead of being excited, they'd then ask me what the tangible benefit of that would be and I'd feel confused and think, "But that is a tangible benefit. Look at how differently the group is behaving. Listen to how differently people talk one another."

To use a metaphor from my mentor, Sarah Smith, people were asking about what kinds of furniture our workshop could produce and wanted me to tell them we made fine wardrobes or comfortable chairs. Instead, I was telling them how well our lathe could cut through wood and how this meant that whatever they wanted could be made to order. It didn't help that most of my early clients had been the kinds of people who knew that the process was the most important part of change. I'd been spoilt in thinking that everyone would be as fascinated by group dynamics as I was.

I had a small pool of systemic modellers to draw on now and we were ready to take on bigger projects because I wouldn't have lead them all myself. I wanted associates to be able to say clearly what people could hope to get from having us in their organisations. I didn't just want sound bites, I wanted to say meaningful things that I felt congruent with.

I reviewed previous projects and the kinds of information gathered so far. I was already aware that evaluation had been sporadic, and was often carried out without the support of our clients, without a budget and relying on our own initiative and the data available to us. Even having Nancy, a full-time chartered occupational psychologist, on board, with all her keen intelligence and knowledge of the field, hadn't enabled us to carry out much meaningful, rigorous research to the level that we'd hoped.

It is always a source of amazement to me how much public and private money is spent on change processes and initiatives without there being investment into tracking that change over the short and medium term.

However the kinds of research we had done can be illustrated using a simple model I developed with a consultancy client, Eli Rebeiro of Delta7 Change Ltd.

Four Quadrants to Evidence Change

The evidence for the impact of our work came from a variety of sources and Eli and I separated these into four quadrants to help us understand the differences between them:

Quadrant 1: Stories, quotes and anecdotal evidence.
Quadrant 2: Questionnaires, surveys and semi structured interviews.
Quadrant 3: Observable behavioural differences in the groups while they were working.
Quadrant 4: Tangible shifts in output.

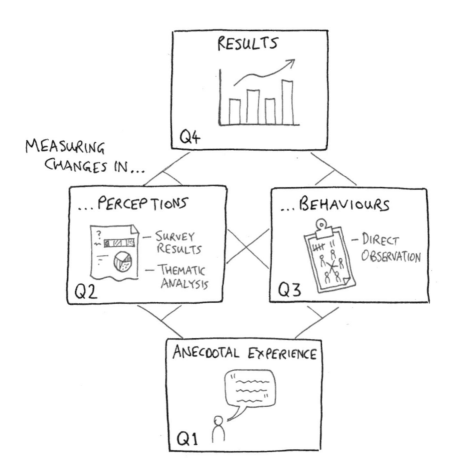

Quadrant 1: Stories, quotes and anecdotal evidence

This quadrant is filled with the things people say from a personal perspective about the difference the work has made to them. This may be sound-bites from interviews or quotes from debrief sessions at the end of a project. While completely subjective, these quotes often capture life-changing insights or dramatic improvements at work as a result of our intervention. They are great for sharing potential benefits with prospective clients:

- Clean Language is like putting Dyno-Rod® through our communication channels.
- This has helped us to reflect on our people as effectively as we reflect our processes.
- It's the first diversity training course where I didn't feel I was being discriminated against.
- I'm less inclined to rescue my staff team and more inclined to trust that they can sort out their own issues.

This is clearly a useful quadrant with lots of valuable information but it doesn't really let us know what happened to create those experiences.

Quadrant 2: Questionnaires, surveys and semi-structured interviews

This quadrant is about taking a more systematic approach to subjective experience. It contains notes from semi-structured interviews, results from questionnaires, surveys, ratings and rankings. For example:

- When Nancy and Emma created the six-day Welfare to Work programme for the long-term unemployed, Nancy sent employment advisors a questionnaire with a scale to rate their clients on job readiness before and after their peer coaching course. This allowed her to say with confidence that employment advisors judged their clients as moving an average of five points on the job readiness scale.

- During the diversity project we interviewed clients before, during and after the training. We asked about their thoughts and perceptions and then analysed these interview transcripts for patterns.

The information gathered during these semi-structured interviews, using clean questions to elaborate people's answers, is quite robust because the clean-ness of the questions can reduce the interviewer bias. Still, this quadrant tells us what people say they do and what they say they think rather than providing evidence about whether they are actually doing anything differently.

Quadrant 3: Observable behavioural differences in the groups while they are working

This third quadrant is all about direct observation: the tangible, observable changes in the dynamics between people in the group, such as:

- Observing two business leaders and registering how many times they made assumptions that didn't make logical sense within the context.
- Counting how many times one member of a group talked over another.
- Noticing whether a group looked directly at one another or towards one group leader.
- Observing a group catch themselves asking dirty questions and laughingly clean them up.

My attention was naturally drawn to this quadrant, as it was this kind of evidence that let me know that my work with any particular client was done.

Quadrant 4: Tangible shifts in output

This is the quadrant that many people are focusing on when they first approach us. They want to know the tangible, objective shifts they can expect in the outputs of their team, organisation or community. What will be the benefit if they bring us in? The tricky thing about this quadrant is that we could point to changes but it was a very different matter trying to explain which changes were directly caused by our interventions. We could say that:

- 60% of the young people in the youth project were in school by the end of nine months.
- The number of pupils at the whole school project achieving five A-C grades had risen from 23% to 43%.
- The percentage of students at the university achieving the top two degree classifications had risen from 49% to 73% since we introduced the self-modelling programme.

But we didn't have any control groups to indicate whether it was our intervention which had made the difference. We also didn't have the in-depth research to indicate which aspect of our approach was the difference that made the difference. We weren't able to identify the 'active ingredient'. We could really only say that we'd done some stuff and some things changed and they may or may not be related. I was at pains to say over and over that we couldn't guarantee results and that there was no research linking our specific process to these results.

The thing that I could say consistently, was that the group dynamics changed and that people started doing and saying different things. These behaviour changes, in-the-moment, must be where the magic happened. There was still something in Quadrant 3 that kept flickering in my peripheral vision, something I wasn't yet able to articulate.

I'd like to share how the final piece of this puzzle fell into place and the moment that I realised I was ready to write this book.

CHAPTER 9

Creating a Network
of Attention

*Developing collaborative team skills in a
fast moving consumer goods company*

I had been developing a relationship with two senior managers of a Fast Moving Goods Company (FMGC) company for over seven years before I was invited to pitch to their business. Sometimes it takes that much Clean Scoping before there is an opportunity for real change. I met Karen and Jayne on open Clean Language training courses and we'd had a series of scoping conversations that had always ended up with us agreeing that they didn't have influence to make a real difference to their Senior Management Team (SMT) culture.

Then, one day, their CEO made a small training budget available and invited members of the SMT to make use of it in whatever way they wanted. A group of interested managers formed a Training Steering Group (TSG) and they agreed to invite three training organisations they knew of to pitch for the training and they'd vote for the one they wanted. This was the 'in' they'd been waiting for and we agreed to pitch.

I proposed that we should be the first company to go in as our pitch would help them to clarify their outcomes and outputs from the training. This would support them to choose the best training company for their needs – a much higher value to me than actually winning the business.

They agreed. Nancy and I turned up, and I asked: "If this training were to go really well for you, it'll be like what?"

There were blank faces and silence. I held the space and asked, "When you've got the first training budget you've had in over ten years, what would you like to have happen?"

The Head of R&D started the ball rolling and said they needed more training in IT systems and Jayne, who was the Head of Marketing, immediately rolled her eyes. I noticed the eye rolling and asked the group, "Who wants something different?" and brought my attention to Jayne, who said:

Jayne: Oh it's nothing to do with IT, it's to do with the communication between us. It's all to do with the way that we operate. We're supposed to be a leadership team and we never speak to each other."

Caitlin: **And for you,** it's to do with communications, **and you'd like** more training in IT ... **Who would like something different?**

I started modelling the contributions from different managers in the group. There were a variety of issues raised, including: lack of teamwork; fire fighting; working in silos; and not trusting one another.

Towards the end of our pitch, one head of department said, "The thing is, I don't think I really want us to change. Because if *we* change, *everything* has to change, and I think actually that might be too difficult for me. I like a quiet life."

They shared some quite revealing conversations and I felt that we'd done a good job getting them to face up to deep divisions in their outcomes and to think more deeply about what they wanted as a group. By going into the sales pitch without an outcome, we'd been able to pay exquisite attention to the group, to their outcomes and to the group dynamics. I felt sure we'd be better placed to serve them as a result. This is an example of the ego-less leadership that seems so crucial to the success of this work.

> By going into the sales pitch without an outcome, we'd been able to pay exquisite attention to the group, to their outcomes and to the group dynamics.

From the discussions we'd heard, Nancy and I identified three issues that they all agreed needed to be addressed:

- They felt stressed and all the fire-fighting meant they were often unable to manage their state at work.

- Their meetings were often problem-focussed without ever arriving at a solution.
- They rarely, if ever, gave feedback to one another and therefore had no access to peer support or peer challenge.

We proposed that a small group of Senior Managers would go through a three-day Systemic Modelling™ programme to use the tools with one another and their own teams and to address these issues internally. Then we'd co-design and co-deliver a second wave of training to the next layer of management.

After they'd seen the other two training pitches they looked at their notes, reflected on their outcomes and chose us. Although a few of them thought it was an odd pitch, they agreed they got more out of our session than any of the others and our proposal was accepted.

We knew we wanted to evaluate this piece of work and made sure we started as early as possible to get our 'before' and 'after' measurements. We were very lucky to have secured the support of Dr Paul Tosey from the Surrey School of Management to help with our design and the writing and publishing of an article.

We sent out the usual Metaphors at Work preparation questions and followed these up with one-to-one interviews or modelling sessions with each of the TSG as well as the four members of the board.

Quadrants 2 and 3: Subjective as well as observed data

To get our Quadrant 3 data, we wanted examples of people doing what they usually did in a group at work. This organisation held 'Category Team Meetings' where members from different functions, such as research and development, packaging, sales etc. came together to co-manage a product, keeping it at the front of supermarket shelves and making a profit. We got observers to sit in the meeting and tally a range of behavioural patterns, including incidences of:

- Closed questions
- Open questions
- Positive instructions

- Negative instructions
- Problem focus
- Outcome focus
- Positive feedback
- Negative feedback
- Questions put to the whole group
- Questions put to an individual person
- Requests for clarification
- Agenda items completed on time

For our Quadrant 2 data, we sent out a company-wide staff survey to get staff to rate themselves and the organisation and to give their opinions on what was working well and what wasn't. We also took the transcripts of the initial semi-structured interviews with the senior managers and analysed them for themes.

We collated all of this Quadrant 3 and Quadrant 2 data and we brought it all back as feedback to the TSG. We shared some of their metaphors for the current state of the business:

- A series of cogs spinning, some of which are connected to each other, others which are just spinning at really high speeds. They are engines and activities in their own right but aren't connected to other activities which would drive output and successful outcomes on a wider scale. The inability to connect and gain momentum sometimes leads to a feeling of powerlessness and fatigue.
- An oil tanker charting a river, avoiding hitting the sides, other boats and mud banks. Occasionally it gets stuck and then it's really bad. We put all the effort into avoiding the sides. For example, when there's a service issue, all the effort goes into dealing with that issue, but you could still bump into another boat or something else could go badly wrong. Everyone is rushing around trying to solve the problem but not actually dealing with the real issue, which is that the river is too small for the boat and it needs to find open water. Unfortunately all the crew are following maps/charts and compasses when really they just need to look out the window and see what's there. We've got it to a critical level, we operate well for a while but we're not very good at operating when something else throws us off course.

Then we shared their metaphors for how they wanted things to be:

- A winning crew in a rowing boat of eight, pulling at the same time, in the same direction and all going at the same speed, as fast as they can, because if you don't, it doesn't quite work. The oars get in the way or the boat goes to one side and doesn't go straight, and it never completes the race as a winner. Sometimes when we don't win the race we need to go back and work out why we didn't win the race … what happened, what didn't happen, and what we're going to do differently to win next time.
- They [the board] would be like the captain on the ship. They decide on the direction and the crew would do the rest. We're the first officers and we get to decide how to get the ship from A to B on the most efficient route.

This way, we were helping them to feel capable of saying how things were, naming things in a straightforward way and having a common understanding of the business from different perspectives.

We also shared the patterns and themes that had emerged from our observations and the questionnaires:

- No direct feedback whatsoever.
- No incidents of clarification.
- 50% of agenda items in meetings not achieved.
- Much higher problem focus than outcome focus.
- A lot of people feeling stressed and under-valued.
- Lots of fire fighting.

They saw that the patterns they were experiencing as a leadership team were the very same patterns that we could observe in the Category Team Meetings. This prepared the way for them to develop one shared outcome for the kind of training they wanted. They decided to concentrate on the skills of giving and receiving feedback, setting joint outcomes and developing their collaboration skills. They felt that once they had these things embedded as good habits then lots of other changes could follow.

We ran the Systemic Modelling™ training with the TSG, utilising all the models you've seen in this book. It was one day a week for three weeks with time in between to practise and develop six metaphor models to encourage emergent knowledge.

After the basic training, we invited the managers to a fourth day where they would bring some live business issues and apply the different processes to them. They wanted to demonstrate to the wider management group that these tools were worth learning. Some of the insights astonished the group. Bobby decided he would take a problem which had proved to be an intractable issue for years. He would think about how to reduce the amount of waste produced as a result of miscalculations in supply and demand. The company had accepted the waste as just a function of the FMCG industry, but he wanted to revisit it.

- He placed the problem in the centre of the room and we used David Grove's Clean Space process to help him to find six different perspectives on the issue.
- When he was standing on the third space, he realised that there was no way what they had been doing would work.
- He had an insight at the fourth space that it was to do with which people were trying to tackle the problem at the same time.
- Then at the fifth space he had a big 'Eureka' moment. He realised which people in the company needed to come together and tackle the problem as a group.
- And from the sixth position he was already working out who he would invite and when. He decided to call the project 'Eureka'.

Later on, he said "Well we were thinking of inviting you up to facilitate the Eureka project, but then we realised you'd just ask, "What would you like to have happen, what is happening and what will you do next?" and we can do that for ourselves now." This was music to my ears and a reminder of how simple this core concept of Systemic Modelling™ is.

Next, together with the TSG, we designed and co-delivered three more days of training to the next level of managers in the organisation. We created a staff training book based on the one we'd created for the university, using the outputs from the TSG training to populate the workbook with quotes and tips from their own leaders about how they were putting the models into action. This made the workbooks more home-grown and branded and also served as a convincer that these tools were being put into use at the highest levels.

Different models were adopted by different leaders and in turn by their management teams. Once a team could experience the benefit they had no difficulty taking on these quite unusual ways of interacting. For example, the Drama Triangle proved very popular with most teams and people could regularly be heard asking whether someone was in drama or not. One team made little flags with P (persecutor), V (victim) and R (rescuer) on them and when they heard a drama statement in a meeting they would raise a flag and everyone would notice and laugh and start the statement again in a Karma way.

In one main office, a whole drama had kicked off amongst the administrative support team and people were coming individually to the head of admin to ask her to take sides or to try and sort it out for them. She went to the front of the office and wrote across the white board:

- What is it that each of you would really like to have happen?
- To achieve this, what will you personally need to do?
- Discuss this and then come to me when you've agreed your plan.

She said she walked out to lunch and when she got back everyone was sitting working together to reorganise the layout of the office so that it didn't lead to the same disputes. They reported that they'd moved from complaining about what they didn't want towards saying what they did want and then it turned out they were all in agreement.

In one of the factories, where delays in the handover process wasted time and decreased productivity, each side of the handover had been blaming the other and thinking that the other held them in contempt. One of the managers called a joint meeting to unpack the problem using the Clean Set Up. They asked each other:

A: If the handover was going just the way you'd like it to, it would be like what?

B: For the handover to go well, you and your team would need to be like what?

C: What would you like from us to make the handover go better?

During this modelling process there was a sudden realisation that a major sticking point was a form that needed signing off. They realised that it came in at the wrong point in the process and delayed everything. One team member had the insight that it was really two forms in one and that the first half could be handed in earlier and the second half could be handed in on completion and this would save a good half an hour every day. They were so pleased with this discovery. One of them agreed to create a draft form that day, try it the next day and revisit it in next week's meeting. It was the Karma Cycle in motion.

Just as in earlier projects, I was astonished at how easily groups would adopt the models and make new use of them when they were supported by the leaders. One senior manager brought Clean Feedback into every weekly meeting. He wrote the model on a white board and said to his whole team (only two of whom had done the training):

"I'm going to run today's meeting and I'd like the left hand side of the room to give me feedback on the content of the meeting, what's working well, what isn't working so well for you and what would you prefer to hear about in our next meeting. The right hand side of the room to give me feedback on the structure of the meeting. For you personally, let me know what works well, what doesn't work so well and what you'd like me to do differently next week."

He reported back to the training group, "You could have heard a pin drop. Everyone was just stunned into silence."

He ran the meeting as usual and at the end he asked for feedback and the two managers who'd been on the training gave him Clean Feedback one on content and one on structure. He asked a couple of questions to clarify what they meant and then thanked them.

The next meeting he did it again, and the next meeting he did it again. He said that by the third week, other people from the team were giving their feedback too and following the model.

This was a beautiful example of a senior manager modelling the skills and attitudes out in the moment and everybody else getting the meta-message that this is the way we're going to do things around here.

At this stage in the project we gathered some Quadrant 1 sound bites and heard just the kinds of things we were used to:

- The training has woken us up and made us aware that we are working together and everyone is on the same boat.

- Silo mentality has been eroded.
- When anyone speaks there's less drama, a lot more conversation. I notice it in meetings. They are amazingly calm; we're all together and we know we are.
- More of the previously unspeakable issues are coming out in meetings rather than corridors.

But we'd reached the end of the training budget and we were still at the pilot stage. We hadn't had contact with enough senior or middle managers to reach a tipping point and create a full-scale culture change. A new CEO was appointed at this time, who was much less facilitative, much more of a 'command and control' leader who didn't approve of self-organising staff. These processes were contrary to the way he wanted staff to work. Still we were pleased with what we'd seen and heard so far and decided to be happy to find out what was possible from such a small scale intervention. Nine months later we went back to observe the groups again and to re-interview the TSG and those who'd been involved in the training. I was really interested to know whether any of those initial changes would still be in evidence.

The Quadrant 2 results, where people reported their subjective experience and we measured changes, were promising:

- All the senior managers who were interviewed reported that they were still better able to manage their state at work and to respond more appropriately under stress.
- 86% reported being more outcome-focused.
- 93% reported that they were giving and receiving feedback more frequently.

These were the three themes that had been identified by the SMT as areas that needed improvement – for the business it meant having managers who were in a better state to rise to challenges, give feedback that made a difference and steer themselves and their teams away from blame and towards practical solutions. This result was an initial success in terms of changing people's reported experience.

With regard to how people felt about working with colleagues who had also completed the training, again the Quadrant 2 figures were good:

- 93% reported that they were engaging in greater challenge, discussion and deeper thinking
- 79% were experiencing greater trust and collaboration with peers
- 86% had noticed less blame and more positive conflict resolution

We could also gather Quadrant 1 quotes and anecdotes to give us descriptions of their internal experience:

- Within the small group of us who did the training we get on and solve problems more quickly – there's a lot more appreciation of different areas of the business which means there's less blame.

... and how the training had helped them cope with a new CEO and a big change in culture:

- If we'd not had that team building experience we'd be pulling each other apart by now.

Originally the proposal was intended to move from the pilot to a more extensive training programme. We'd hoped to work with 100% of senior managers and 70% of middle managers and so far we had trained 50% of senior managers and only 30% of middle managers. My attention was very much on whether, with such a small spread of training, there'd been any change in the Quadrant 3 behaviours in the Category Team Meetings at all.

I went in and observed a cross section of meetings as we had in the beginning. The first group I observed gave me a bit of a shock. As people arrived nobody smiled or talked to one another. There was no banter, no energy, no signs of enjoyment across the whole meeting. The chair simply said, "Right, let's start." And as he read through each agenda point the relevant person would say yes they'd done it or no they hadn't. Nobody clarified anything or said anything other than a few monotone words. I thought I was losing the will to live. It was an example of meetings at their worst: long, tedious and meaningless, just like we'd observed before the start of the project.

The next group was very different but almost as bad. One chairperson controlled all the interactions. She took the first agenda item and, looking at the relevant person, she asked:

Chair: Right, have you done this?

A: No.

Chair: Well you have to get it done. That's not good enough.

A: OK.

Chair: *(To minute-taker)* We'll have to push that deadline back.
            (To group) What's next?

Again there was no inquiry or challenge or real learning across the group. No positive feedback, all questions directed to a single person rather than to the group as a whole.

There were people in those meetings who'd been using clean questions and the Karma Cycle fluently only a few months previously and now they were as miserable and unproductive as ever.

I felt so sad; what a waste of our time and their money and all the hope those people had had during the training.

The third meeting, however, was like a breath of fresh air. The attendees arrived and were chatting to each other. The chair said, "Right, here's the first agenda point. What are the actions on this?" And they all discussed it, sharing ideas, sharing things that had worked in other parts of the business, putting forward proposals, clarifying what was meant and suggesting things they could do next. The chair summarised what had been said and checked who was going to do what and by when. Then she went on to the next point.

I had an observation sheet full of tallies for open questions, positive instruction, group level questions and quick switches from problem to outcome focus but I wasn't sure what had made this meeting so different. Was one product so much more interesting than another? I must have been missing something.

The fourth meeting was chaired by the same person who'd run the dire first meeting so I expected it to be awful again. Instead, although this chairperson wasn't particularly good at summarising and taking each agenda item from problem to action, the meeting was still really good. All the members of the group were sharing, challenging each other and giving one another feedback. It was lively, full of learning, positive instruction and outcome focussed.

The rest of the meetings I observed continued in this pattern. Some were dire, dull and listless, some were run 'command and control' style, while others were lively, communicative, making use of all of the members of the meeting and arriving at agreed outcomes and actions.

The most remarkable observation for me was that someone might behave appallingly in one meeting – being dull, disengaged and belligerent – and *the same person* in a 'good' meeting would be fun, chatty, collaborative and take full responsibility for getting things done. It was like they were two different people.

In the dire meetings there was no change from the results that we'd seen before the project. Still around 50% of agenda items were completed on time and 50% had to be delayed and there was virtually no group learning at all.

In the lively meetings there was a 50% increase in the number of agenda items being completed to time, which was now at 75%. We could see and hear lots of feedback, challenge and clarification and most questions were open and addressed to the whole group. They were great examples of people collaborating to resolve issues.

As I went through the observation sheets, I noticed some doodles I had made when I was tracking the behaviours. I'd drawn a circle for the group and crosses for each person. Then every time someone spoke, I had drawn a line from them to the person they were talking to and along that line marked if it was an open or a closed question. If the question was made to the group as a whole I drew a line into the centre of the circle and then drew a line into that point from everyone who contributed to answering the query. This meant that I'd absent-mindedly drawn the shape of the dynamics in the meeting...

In the dull and boring meetings the interactions looked a bit like this: The chair would ask one question of a specific person – and that person would answer. Then the questioning stopped. Another person in the group might ask a closed question of a specific colleague, that colleague would say yes or no, then the interaction stopped. It was like a lacklustre pinball machine with no bounce and there were always some people who made no contribution at all.

In the few dire meetings with a very strong chair, there was a very different shape. All interactions went from a central part to a specific person. There were no questions to the centre of the group and all people answered directly to the chair. I've been calling this 'Command and Control'.

With the lively meetings there was a completely different shape happening. Nearly all comments went to the centre of the group and at least three people would comment on each topic. It started to build up this shape:

In these meetings everyone contributed in an equal way and as the meeting progressed, any problem or issue was put to the whole group. A number of people would propose ideas or ask questions to build up a group sense of what was going on and what could happen differently. By challenging one another or asking for clarification, an even stronger network of attention was formed. Every single member spoke, not only to specific people but to the group as a whole. Here's an example of an interaction from one of these 'star' meetings:

Chair: Let's start with bleach. What's happening with this?
Sales: We're really wanting to see examples of the new brand. Marketing, are they ready?

Marketing: No I'm afraid we haven't had the prototypes from packaging yet.
Chair: Packaging, what's happened?
Packaging: Oh, the person in charge of the project was off sick for two weeks with swine flu so it wasn't done.
Sales: What's your sickness policy to keep on top of projects?
Packaging: We don't have one.
Sales: We've started one that means every project has a second in command, just in case someone goes off sick, they can pick up the project or at the very least let everyone else in category know so that there isn't an unexpected hold up. We've been using it for about four months.
Chair: Anyone else got a good sickness contingency plan?
R and D: We use the same one as Sales; one of our team came up with it.
Chair: Packaging, what would have to happen for you to implement this?
Packaging: I'd have to get my head of department involved.
Sales: Would you like me to get my head to raise it at the next SMT so that we're all using the same contingency plan?
Packaging: That would be great. In the meantime I can get to these specific samples myself today and get them down to you by the end of the week.
Chair: Right, on this occasion we've had to push this back due to illness but Sales you'll get your head to raise it at the SMT on Monday and Packaging will you report back to us what changes are made?

These teams were actively moving their problems through the Karma Cycle and agreeing actions before they moved on to the next point. This was resulting in a lovely star shaped network around the themes, in this case; packaging samples and sickness policy. And the group seemed inspired to take problems as they arose, explore and resolve them and move on with a sense of fun and happy energy, so different from the meetings with command and control or pinball shapes.

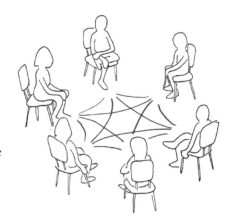

What started as doodles became one of the most effective tools I've developed to demonstrate Quadrant 3 changes. With this new model I could observe any meeting and map out the dynamics, and assess whether the shape of the meeting was fit for purpose. If the purpose of the meeting was to give out information and control staff then command and control was fine. But if the purpose was to bring together experts to share knowledge and design collaborative solutions then a star meeting could be a better form. I could also feedback whether the people representing certain areas of the business were being over or under-utilised in these meetings by how many contributions they made.

I was thrilled with my new tool for analysing the shape of interactions in a group and started thinking back to other projects I'd run and back to the very first youth project and could see that this change in group dynamics had been happening then but I hadn't had a model to explain it. I used to turn my own hand upside down with each finger representing a child to show how the children paid attention to one another around the group to grow and learn.

Within the FMCG, I used my doodles to feed back to the meeting chairs the shapes of the meetings they'd been running. They could see how the Karma Cycle could be put to practical use to keep the group's attention on an outcome and stay with it until they moved it to action.

What we didn't know, in terms of this client and this data, was why some meetings were so different from others, especially given that they often contained the same people. Nancy and I pored over the data and then she spotted a pattern. In the lively star meetings, over 50% of the people had attended the three-day Systemic Modelling™ training. In contrast, in the pinball or command and control style meetings, fewer than 50% of people had attended the training. It seemed that when enough trained people got together it changed the shape of the attention in the group.

People who were using the tools skilfully in star meetings didn't use them at all in meetings where they were in the minority. It wasn't down to a change in a specific individual. It was down to a change at a group level. This was quite a revelation at first but then as I thought back to past projects, I realise that this had always been a pattern. It was one of those things that I knew instinctively, but was not consciously articulating it.

I'd already been saying to previous clients that around 60% of people needed to undergo or be influenced by the training to achieve the crucial tipping point for it to become 'the way we do things around here' in the organisation. We were now seeing in a microcosm what we'd observed across whole organisations. There needed to be at least 50% of the people in the meeting operating in the new way for the culture of a meeting to change.

The last piece of the puzzle fell into place. Now I could understand what it was that I was looking for in Quadrant 3 that I hadn't been able to articulate. The big change in the groups couldn't be seen just by classifying and counting interactions, it was to do with the shape of the network of attention that a group was creating. The attention across the system or group needed to become more of a network or a star. This group level shift in attention demonstrated they were self-modelling; utilising the skills and experience of the various people to create insights and emergent knowledge that they couldn't have had on their own.

It made so much sense; I hadn't been designing an intervention to achieve a specific goal, I had been designing a process to create more collaborative groups. This was why it was so important never to take the expert position in the group. I didn't want their attention on me; I wanted them attending to one another. I didn't control the dynamic of the group, I tracked it, fed it back to them and asked them what they wanted to have happen. My job was to inspire them to feel capable of paying the same quality of attention to one another so that they didn't need me anymore. I had discovered how to create the conditions for a group to become a compassionate and passionate self-modelling system. It was time to stop doing and time to start writing. I needed to share what I knew.

Postscript

I think David Grove would have loved my doodles of group dynamics and the emergence of star meetings as the result of Systemic Modelling™. He'd have challenged me to start looking for patterns in nature that correlated or contradicted my findings. As always, he'd have been deeply compassionate and endlessly curious. But, after the university project and before I found the missing piece of the puzzle, David died, suddenly.

There was a wave of shock and grief across the clean community and many of us made our way to New Zealand to be with his family and to pay tribute to our friend and mentor. I experienced an extraordinary sense of loss and I hadn't realised until he was gone, how much of what I was doing, I did with him in mind. Wondering what he'd say or think and wanting him to be proud of what I was doing with his work. I missed being with someone who gave me the attention, time and space I needed not only to be myself, but to discover who else I could be.

But he left a huge legacy: his own work and all the work of others who have been inspired by him. My contribution to this legacy is Systemic Modelling™: clean language for groups, teams and organisations. With this simple set of models we can make a huge difference to the quality of attention we pay to ourselves and to others. We have an approach for creating the time and space that we need to connect and to collaborate – a process for inspiring capability in ourselves, and in one another, to move away from contempt, towards curiosity, compassion and love.

So that more of us are able to be at our best, much more of the time.

APPENDIX I

What would you like to have happen next?

I guess the answer to this question depends on where your attention has been while reading the book.

If you'd like to start a **discussion with Caitlin** on applications, projects or research, you can email her at: **caitlin@trainingattention.co.uk**

If you'd like to **read more about applications for Systemic Modelling**™ you can find further case studies at: **www.trainingattention.co.uk.**

If you'd like to get some **training in Clean Language, Symbolic Modelling or Systemic Modelling**™, please visit **www.cleanlearning.co.uk** to find a course or a practice group or an introductory teleseminar to begin your learning journey.

If you'd like to **use Clean Language** or **Systemic Modelling**™ in your own practice please reference David John Grove as the originator of Clean Language, Clean Space and Emergent Knowledge and the source of all of this wonderful work. Please reference Penny Tompkins and James Lawley as the developers of Symbolic Modelling. And finally, please reference Caitlin Walker as the developer of Systemic Modelling™. The sources of specific models and the people who contributed to them can be found in Appendix II.

Above all, I encourage you to use these tools to pay exquisite attention to yourself, to others and to the groups you interact with so that more of you are able to be at your best more of the time.

APPENDIX II

Sourcing the Concepts, Models & Development of Systemic Modelling™

Even though I endeavoured not to study any theories as I journeyed along my compelling path, I spent those years working and conversing with people more experienced and widely read than myself and they naturally introduced me to models that influenced my thinking. If you'd like to discover more about the models and the work of the people who contributed to them, I recommend you look up the authors and find their latest publications.

Systemic Modelling™ Models

- **Clean Feedback** Original Concept: Dee Berridge and Caitlin Walker, 1997; Evolution 1: Caitlin Walker and Nancy Doyle, 2008; Evolution 2: Caitlin Walker, 2012
- **Clean Scoping** Caitlin Walker, 2012
- **Clean Set Up** Dee Berridge and Caitlin Walker, 1997
- **Developmental Tasks** Dee Berridge and Caitlin Walker, 1997
- **Drama to Karma** Nancy Doyle and Caitlin Walker, 2005
- **Four Quadrants of Evaluation** Caitlin Walker and Eli Rebeiro, 2012
- **Karma Cycle** Combination of ideas and iterations from Dee Berridge, Caitlin Walker, Nancy Doyle, and Marian Way
- **Metaphors at Work** Caitlin Walker, 2000
- **Systemic Modelling™ Star** Caitlin Walker, 1998 - 2010
- **When You're _____ at Your Best** Dee Berridge and Caitlin Walker, 1997

Other Models we use in Systemic Modelling™

- **Clean Language, Clean Space and Emergent Knowledge** David Grove, 1980s - 2008
- **I'm OK, You're OK** Thomas A Harris MD, 1967 (introduced to me by Chris Grimsley)
- **Karpman Triangle (Drama Triangle)** Stephen Karpman, M.D. © 1967-2008, 2011
- **Problem, Remedy, Outcome (PRO)** Penny Tompkins and James Lawley, 2006 (see www.cleanlanguage.co.uk)
- **Triune Brain** Dr Paul MacLean, 1960

Background Reading / Resources

- **Clean Approaches for Coaches** Marian Way, 2013
- **Clean Language and Systemic Modelling™ (DVD)** Caitlin Walker, 2011
- **Metaphors in Mind** James Lawley and Penny Tompkins, 2000
- **Resolving Traumatic Memories: Metaphors and Symbols in Psychotherapy** David J. Grove and B. I. Panzer, 1989
- **The Power of Six** Philip Harland, 2012
- **Trust Me, I'm The Patient** Philip Harland, 2009

Index

About the Author

After graduating in Linguistics at the School of Oriental and African Studies, Caitlin completed four years post-graduate research in 'Strategies for Lexical Access' including fieldwork in Ghana. To support her studies she worked as a barmaid, cleaner, subject of psychological experiments and youth worker in an inner city community garden. She was introduced to David Grove, originator of Clean Language, in the late 1990s and as well as developing her skills in one-to-one therapy, she began to devise group level applications for his work.

Caitlin Walker

She became a tutor in a central government funded project to work with groups of at-risk young people with the aim of keeping them within mainstream education. During this time she developed her unique approach to using Clean Language as a process for creating a self-modelling culture across the group. Rather than teaching the young people from an expert position, she facilitated them to become peer coaches. They could then use their diverse experiences and strengths to support one another to transform their learning and behaviour.

Caitlin took her approach and worked over 15 years to make it transferable, scalable and teachable and has come to call it Systemic Modelling™. She has designed and delivered bespoke projects addressing: public sector diversity training; police interview training; conflict and mediation; ethical sales practice; accelerated learning; increasing student attainment; recruitment and retention; family mediation; and managing change and transition in all sectors.

She works and trains internationally and can also be found at home, in her garden, enjoying time with her husband, three children, her dog and her chickens.